The Easy
Crock Pot

Cookbook
---
for Beginners

2000 Days of Simple and Healthy Slow-Cooker Recipes to Nourish Your Body and Delight Your Taste Buds—With Easy Prep and Stress-Free Cooking

Scott Gonzalez

Table of Contents

INTRODUCTION

Rediscovering the Art of Slow Cooking

In a world where everything moves at a fast pace, there is something profoundly comforting about the slow and steady process of cooking with a Crock Pot. This humble appliance, often nestled in a corner of the kitchen, has the remarkable ability to transform simple ingredients into rich, flavorful dishes, all while requiring minimal effort from the cook. If you're someone who appreciates the joys of home-cooked meals but struggles to find the time to prepare them, this Crock Pot Cookbook is your new best friend.

Slow cooking is not a new concept. For centuries, people have relied on low and slow methods to tenderize tough cuts of meat, extract flavors from spices and herbs, and create hearty, nourishing meals that feed both body and soul. The Crock Pot, with its simple yet effective design, brings this age-old technique into the modern kitchen, allowing anyone to create delicious meals with ease.

The Magic of Hands-Free Cooking

The beauty of the Crock Pot lies in its simplicity. You don't need to be a culinary expert or spend hours in the kitchen to create delicious meals. All you need are a few basic ingredients, a little bit of preparation, and the patience to let time do the work for you. The Crock Pot allows you to "set it and forget it," giving you the freedom to go about your day while dinner cooks itself.

Whether you're busy at work, juggling family responsibilities, or simply want to spend less time in the kitchen, the Crock Pot makes it easy to enjoy home-cooked meals without the hassle. Just imagine coming home to the inviting aroma of a slow-cooked stew or roast, ready to be served the moment you walk through the door. With the Crock Pot, you can turn that fantasy into a daily reality.

Why Slow Cooking Is Healthier Cooking

One of the greatest advantages of cooking with a Crock Pot is its ability to promote healthier eating habits. Unlike fast-cooking methods that often require added fats, oils, or high heat, slow cooking uses gentle heat over a longer period to extract maximum flavor from your ingredients. This means you can achieve delicious, rich tastes without relying on excessive salt, sugar, or unhealthy fats.

Slow cooking is also ideal for preserving the nutrients in your food. High-heat cooking methods can destroy or diminish the vitamins and minerals in fresh vegetables, lean meats, and legumes. In contrast, the low, steady heat of a Crock Pot helps retain these essential nutrients, ensuring that every meal is as healthy as it is delicious. Whether you're preparing a lean stew packed with vegetables or a protein-rich chili, you can feel good knowing that you're serving your family nutritious food.

Simplicity Meets Versatility

The Crock Pot is one of the most versatile tools you can have in your kitchen. It's perfect for preparing a wide range of dishes, from comforting soups and stews to flavorful curries, casseroles, and even desserts. But its versatility goes beyond just the types of meals you can prepare. It's also incredibly flexible in terms of timing. Whether you have all day or just a few hours, there's a Crock Pot setting that suits your schedule.

Unlike other kitchen appliances that require constant monitoring, the Crock Pot allows you to cook without worry. You can load it up in the morning, set it to low, and come back eight hours later to a perfectly cooked dinner. Alternatively, if you're short on time, you can use the high setting for faster results. This flexibility makes it ideal for any lifestyle, whether you're a busy professional, a parent managing a household, or someone who simply enjoys the art of slow cooking.

Minimal Effort, Maximum Flavor

One of the great pleasures of Crock Pot cooking is how effortlessly it brings out the best in your ingredients. The slow, gentle heat breaks down the fibers in meats, making them incredibly tender and juicy. Vegetables absorb all the flavors of the broth, herbs, and spices, creating a depth of taste that's hard to achieve with quick-cooking methods.

This approach is especially beneficial for those who love rich, hearty flavors but don't want to spend hours in the kitchen. With a Crock Pot, you can make restaurant-quality dishes with minimal effort. There's no need for constant stirring, monitoring, or adjusting heat levels. The Crock Pot does all the work, allowing you to enjoy delicious, flavorful meals with none of the stress.

Economical Cooking for Every Budget

Cooking with a Crock Pot isn't just about convenience and taste — it's also about saving money. Because slow cooking tenderizes tougher cuts of meat, you don't need to buy the most expensive ingredients to create a fantastic meal. In fact, some of the most flavorful Crock Pot dishes are made with economical cuts like chuck roast, pork shoulder, or chicken thighs.

Additionally, the Crock Pot is perfect for batch cooking and meal prepping. You can easily make a large batch of soup, stew, or chili and store the leftovers in the refrigerator or freezer for later. This not only saves time but also reduces food waste and cuts down on your grocery bills. With a Crock Pot, you can enjoy delicious, home-cooked meals without breaking the bank.

A Tool for Every Cook

Whether you're a novice cook just starting out or a seasoned chef looking to simplify your routine, the Crock Pot is a tool that everyone can benefit from. For beginners, it offers a forgiving way to learn basic cooking techniques and experiment with new flavors without the risk of burning or overcooking your food. For experienced cooks, it's an opportunity to explore more complex recipes and refine your slow-cooking skills.

This cookbook is designed to help you make the most out of your Crock Pot, no matter your level of expertise. You'll find a range of recipes that are easy to follow and adaptable to your taste preferences and dietary needs. From family favorites to new and exciting dishes, this book will inspire you to get creative in the kitchen and discover all the possibilities of slow cooking.

Your Crock Pot Adventure Begins Here

So, are you ready to dive into the world of Crock Pot cooking? This cookbook will be your guide, offering a collection of delicious, easy-to-make recipes that are perfect for any occasion. Whether you're cooking for a crowd or just for yourself, you'll find recipes that are sure to impress.

As you explore the recipes in this book, you'll learn how to master the art of slow cooking, develop your own signature dishes, and most importantly, enjoy the process. Cooking should be a joy, not a chore, and with the Crock Pot, it can be exactly that.

So, grab your Crock Pot, gather your ingredients, and let's start cooking. Your culinary adventure is just a page away. Welcome to the wonderful world of Crock Pot cooking, where great meals are made with love and patience, one slow, delicious step at a time.

Chapter 1

Breakfasts

Egg–Potato Bake

Prep time: 20 minutes | Cook time: 6 hours | Serves 2

- 2 slices bacon, chopped
- 1 cup pork sausage
- 1 onion, chopped
- 1 cup sliced button mushrooms
- 2 garlic cloves, minced
- 1 orange bell pepper, chopped
- Nonstick cooking spray
- 3 russet potatoes, peeled and sliced
- 1 cup shredded Havarti cheese
- ½ cup shredded Colby cheese
- 5 eggs, beaten
- 1 cup milk
- ½ teaspoon salt
- ½ teaspoon dried thyme leaves
- ⅛ teaspoon freshly ground black pepper

1. In a medium skillet over medium heat, cook the bacon and sausage until the bacon is crisp and the sausage is browned, 10 minutes or so, stirring frequently. Remove the bacon and sausage to a paper towel–lined plate to drain. Remove and discard all but 1 tablespoon of drippings from the pan. 2. In the same skillet over medium heat, cook the onion, mushrooms, and garlic in the remaining drippings until tender, about 5 minutes. Remove from the heat and add the bell pepper, bacon, and sausage. 3. Line the crock pot with heavy-duty foil and spray with the nonstick cooking spray. 4. In the crock pot, layer the potatoes, bacon mixture, and cheeses. 5. In a medium bowl, beat the eggs, milk, salt, thyme, and pepper. Pour the egg mixture into the crock pot. 6. Cover and cook on low for 6 hours, or until the temperature reaches 160ºF (71ºC) on a food thermometer. 7. Using the foil, remove from the crock pot, cut into squares, and serve.

Peach French Toast Bake

Prep time: 15 minutes | Cook time: 6 hours | Serves 2

- Nonstick cooking spray
- ½ cup brown sugar
- 3 tablespoons butter
- 1 tablespoon water
- 1 teaspoon vanilla
- 8 slices French bread
- 1½ cups peeled sliced peaches
- 4 eggs
- 1 cup milk
- ¼ cup granulated sugar
- ½ teaspoon ground cinnamon
- ¼ teaspoon salt
- ⅔ cup chopped pecans

1. Line the crock pot with heavy-duty foil, and spray with the nonstick cooking spray. 2. In a small saucepan over low heat, bring the brown sugar, butter, and water to a simmer. Simmer about 5 minutes, stirring, until the mixture forms a syrup. Remove from the heat and stir in the vanilla. 3. In the crock pot, layer in the bread and the peaches, drizzling each layer with some of the brown sugar syrup. 4. In a medium bowl, beat the eggs, milk, granulated sugar, cinnamon, and salt. Pour the egg mixture into the crock pot and sprinkle with the pecans. 5. Cover and cook on low for 6 hours, or until the temperature registers 160ºF (71ºC) on a food thermometer and the mixture is set. 6. Remove from the crock pot, slice, and serve.

Welsh Rarebit

Prep time: 10 minutes | Cook time: 1½ to 2½ hours | Serves 6 to 8

- 1 (12-ounce / 340-g) can beer
- 1 tablespoon dry mustard
- 1 teaspoon Worcestershire sauce
- ½ teaspoon salt
- ⅛ teaspoon black or white pepper
- 1 pound (454 g) American
- cheese, cubed
- 1 pound (454 g) sharp Cheddar cheese, cubed
- English muffins or toast
- Tomato slices
- Bacon, cooked until crisp
- Fresh steamed asparagus spears

1. In crock pot, combine beer, mustard, 2. Worcestershire sauce, salt, and pepper. Cover and cook on high 1 to 2 hours, until mixture boils. 3. Add cheese, a little at a time, stirring constantly until all the cheese melts. 4. Heat on high 20 to 30 minutes with cover off, stirring frequently. 5. Serve hot over toasted English muffins or over toasted bread cut into triangles. Garnish with tomato slices, strips of crisp bacon and steamed asparagus spears.

Spanakopita Frittata

Prep time: 10 minutes | Cook time: 5 to 6 hours | Serves 8

- 1 tablespoon extra-virgin olive oil
- 12 eggs
- 1 cup heavy (whipping) cream
- 2 teaspoons minced garlic
- 2 cups chopped spinach
- ½ cup feta cheese
- Cherry tomatoes, halved, for garnish (optional)
- Yogurt, for garnish (optional)
- Parsley, for garnish (optional)

1. Lightly grease the insert of the crock pot with the olive oil. 2. In a medium bowl, whisk together the eggs, heavy cream, garlic, spinach, and feta. Pour the mixture into the crock pot. 3. Cover and cook on low 5 to 6 hours. 4. Serve topped with the tomatoes, a dollop of yogurt, and parsley, if desired.

Dulce Leche

Prep time: 5 minutes | Cook time: 2 hours | Makes 2½ cups

- 2 (14-ounce / 397-g) cans sweetened condensed milk
- Cookies, for serving

1. Place unopened cans of milk in crock pot. Fill cooker with warm water so that it comes above the cans by 1½ to 2 inches. 2. Cover cooker. Cook on high 2 hours. 3. Cool unopened cans. 4. When opened, the contents should be thick and spreadable. Use as a filling between 2 cookies.

Crustless Wild Mushroom–Kale Quiche

Prep time: 10 minutes | Cook time: 5 to 6 hours | Serves 8

- 1 tablespoon extra-virgin olive oil
- 12 eggs
- 1 cup heavy (whipping) cream
- 1 tablespoon chopped fresh thyme
- 1 tablespoon chopped fresh chives
- ¼ teaspoon freshly ground black pepper
- ⅛ teaspoon salt
- 2 cups coarsely chopped wild mushrooms (shiitake, portobello, oyster, enoki)
- 1 cup chopped kale
- 1 cup shredded Swiss cheese

1. Lightly grease the insert of the crock pot with the olive oil. 2. In a medium bowl, whisk together the eggs, heavy cream, thyme, chives, pepper, and salt. Stir in the mushrooms and kale. Pour the mixture into the crock pot and top with the cheese. 3. Cover and cook on low 5 to 6 hours. 4. Serve warm.

Mediterranean Eggs

Prep time: 10 minutes | Cook time: 5 to 6 hours | Serves 4

- 1 tablespoon extra-virgin olive oil
- 12 eggs
- ½ cup coconut milk
- ½ teaspoon dried oregano
- ½ teaspoon freshly ground black pepper
- ¼ teaspoon salt
- 2 cups chopped spinach
- 1 tomato, chopped
- ¼ cup chopped sweet onion
- 1 teaspoon minced garlic
- ½ cup crumbled goat cheese

1. Lightly grease the insert of the crock pot with the olive oil. 2. In a large bowl, whisk together the eggs, coconut milk, oregano, pepper, and salt, until well blended. 3. Add the spinach, tomato, onion, and garlic, and stir to combine. 4. Pour the egg mixture into the insert and top with the crumbled goat cheese. 5. Cover and cook on low 5 to 6 hours, until it is set like a quiche. 6. Serve warm.

Granola

Prep time: 15 minutes | Cook time: 4 hours | Makes 8 cups

- Nonstick cooking spray
- 4 cups old-fashioned rolled oats
- 1 cup slivered almonds
- 1 cup coarsely chopped pecans
- 1 cup sunflower seeds
- 1 cup shredded coconut
- ⅓ cup butter or coconut oil
- 2 tablespoons safflower oil
- ½ cup honey
- ⅓ cup brown sugar
- 2 teaspoons vanilla
- 1 teaspoon ground cinnamon
- ½ teaspoon salt

1. Spray the crock pot with the nonstick cooking spray. 2. In the crock pot, combine the oats, almonds, pecans, sunflower seeds, and coconut. 3. In a medium saucepan over low heat, heat the butter, safflower oil, honey, brown sugar, vanilla, cinnamon, and salt until the butter melts, about 5 minutes. 4. Drizzle the butter mixture over the ingredients in the crock pot and stir to coat. 5. Cover, but leave the lid slightly ajar, and cook on low for 3 to 4 hours, stirring every hour if possible, until the mixture is golden brown. 6. Remove the granola to greased baking sheets and spread into an even layer. Let cool, and then break into pieces. Serve or store in an airtight container at room temperature.

Nutty Oatmeal

Prep time: 10 minutes | Cook time: 7 hours | Makes 7 cups

- 1 cup chopped walnuts
- Nonstick cooking spray
- 2 cups rolled oats (not instant or quick cooking)
- 1 cup raisins
- 3 cups almond milk
- 1½ cups apple juice
- ⅓ cup honey
- ⅓ cup brown sugar
- ½ teaspoon ground cinnamon
- ¼ teaspoon ground nutmeg
- ¼ teaspoon salt

1. In a small saucepan over medium-low heat, toast the walnuts until fragrant, about 2 minutes, stirring frequently. 2. Spray the crock pot with the nonstick cooking spray. 3. In the crock pot, combine the walnuts, oats, and raisins. 4. In a large bowl, beat the almond milk, apple juice, honey, brown sugar, cinnamon, nutmeg, and salt. Pour the mixture into the crock pot. 5. Cover and cook on low for 7 hours, or until the oatmeal is thickened and tender, and serve.

Chocolate-Cherry–Stuffed French Toast

Prep time: 15 minutes | Cook time: 6 hours | Serves 2

- Nonstick cooking spray
- 8 slices French bread
- ¾ cup mascarpone cheese
- ½ cup cherry preserves
- ¾ cup semisweet chocolate chips, melted
- 1 cup sliced pitted fresh
- cherries
- 5 eggs, beaten
- 1 cup milk
- 1 teaspoon vanilla
- ½ teaspoon ground cinnamon
- ¼ teaspoon salt

1. Line the crock pot with heavy-duty foil, and spray with the nonstick cooking spray. 2. Spread one side of each slice of bread with the mascarpone cheese and the cherry preserves. Drizzle with the melted chocolate. 3. Cut the bread slices in half and layer them in the crock pot with the fresh cherries. 4. In a medium bowl, beat the eggs, milk, vanilla, cinnamon, and salt. Pour the egg mixture into the crock pot. 5. Cover and cook on low for 6 hours, or until the mixture is set and registers 160°F (71°C) on a food thermometer. Remove from the crock pot using the foil, slice, and serve.

Breakfast Hominy

Prep time: 5 minutes | Cook time: 8 hours | Serves 5

- 1 cup dry cracked hominy
- 1 teaspoon salt
- Black pepper (optional)
- 3 cups water
- 2 tablespoons butter

1. Stir all ingredients together in a greased crock pot. 2. Cover and cook on low 8 hours, or overnight. 3. Serve warm for breakfast.

Pumpkin-Pecan N'Oatmeal

Prep time: 10 minutes | Cook time: 8 hours | Serves 4

- 1 tablespoon coconut oil
- 3 cups cubed pumpkin, cut into 1-inch chunks
- 2 cups coconut milk
- ½ cup ground pecans
- 1 ounce (28 g) plain protein Powder
- 2 tablespoons granulated erythritol
- 1 teaspoon maple extract
- ½ teaspoon ground nutmeg
- ¼ teaspoon ground cinnamon
- Pinch ground allspice

1. Lightly grease the insert of a slower cooker with the coconut oil. 2. Place the pumpkin, coconut milk, pecans, protein powder, erythritol, maple extract, nutmeg, cinnamon, and allspice in the insert. 3. Cover and cook on low for 8 hours. 4. Stir the mixture or use a potato masher to create your preferred texture, and serve.

Slow-Cooked Blueberry French Toast

Prep time: 30 minutes | Cook time: 3 hours | Serves 12

- 8 eggs
- ½ cup plain yogurt
- ⅓ cup sour cream
- 1 teaspoon vanilla extract
- ½ teaspoon ground cinnamon
- 1 cup 2% milk
- ⅓ cup maple syrup
- 1 (1-pound / 454-g) loaf French bread, cubed
- 1½ cups fresh or frozen
- blueberries
- 12 ounces (340 g) cream cheese, cubed
- Blueberry Syrup:
- 1 cup sugar
- 2 tablespoons cornstarch
- 1 cup cold water
- ¾ cup fresh or frozen blueberries, divided
- 1 tablespoon butter
- 1 tablespoon lemon juice

1. In a large bowl, whisk eggs, yogurt, sour cream, vanilla and cinnamon. Gradually whisk in milk and maple syrup until blended. 2. Place half of the bread in a greased 5- or 6-quart crock pot; layer with half of the blueberries, cream cheese and egg mixture. Repeat layers. Refrigerate, covered, overnight. 3. Remove from refrigerator 30 minutes before cooking. Cook, covered, on low 3 to 4 hours or until a knife inserted near the center comes out clean. 4. For syrup, in a small saucepan, mix sugar and cornstarch; stir in water until smooth. Stir in ¼ cup blueberries. Bring to a boil; cook and stir until berries pop, about 3 minutes. Remove from heat; stir in butter, lemon juice and remaining berries. Serve warm with French toast.

Blueberry Fancy

Prep time: 15 minutes | Cook time: 3 to 4 hours | Serves 12

- 1 loaf Italian bread, cubed, divided
- 1 pint blueberries, divided
- 8 ounces (227 g) cream
- cheese, cubed, divided
- 6 eggs
- 1½ cups milk

1. Place half the bread cubes in the crock pot. 2. Drop half the blueberries over top the bread. 3. Sprinkle half the cream cheese cubes over the blueberries. 4. Repeat all 3 layers. 5. In a mixing bowl, whisk together eggs and milk. Pour over all ingredients. 6. Cover and cook on low until the dish is set. 7. Serve.

Pumpkin-Pie Breakfast Bars

Prep time: 15 minutes | Cook time: 3 hours | Makes 8 bars

- Crust:
- 5 tablespoons butter, softened, divided
- ¾ cup unsweetened shredded coconut
- ½ cup almond flour
- ¼ cup granulated erythritol
- Filling:
- 1 (28-ounce / 794-g) can pumpkin purée
- 1 cup heavy (whipping) cream
- 4 eggs
- 1 ounce (28 g) protein powder
- 1 teaspoon pure vanilla extract
- 4 drops liquid stevia
- 1 teaspoon ground cinnamon
- ½ teaspoon ground ginger
- ¼ teaspoon ground nutmeg
- Pinch ground cloves
- Pinch salt

Make the Crust: 1. Lightly grease the bottom of the insert of the crock pot with 1 tablespoon of the butter. 2. In a small bowl, stir together the coconut, almond flour, erythritol, and remaining butter until the mixture forms into coarse crumbs. 3. Press the crumbs into the bottom of the insert evenly to form a crust. Make the Filling: 4. In a medium bowl, stir together the pumpkin, heavy cream, eggs, protein powder, vanilla, stevia, cinnamon, ginger, nutmeg, cloves, and salt until well blended. 5. Spread the filling evenly over the crust. 6. Cover and cook on low for 3 hours. 7. Uncover and let cool for 30 minutes. Then place the insert in the refrigerator until completely chilled, about 2 hours. 8. Cut into squares and store them in the refrigerator in a sealed container for up to 5 days.

Cinnamon Buns

Prep time: 20 minutes | Cook time: 1½ hours | Serves 10 to 12

- Buns:
- 6 tablespoons unsalted butter, room temperature, plus more for brushing
- 1⅓ cups warm water (about 110ºF / 43ºC)
- 1 tablespoon active dry yeast
- 2 tablespoons honey
- 3½ cups all-purpose flour, plus more for work surface
- 2 teaspoon coarse salt
- ¾ cup granulated sugar
- ¼ cup plus 2 tablespoons packed brown sugar
- 1 tablespoon ground cinnamon
- Glaze:
- 3 cups confectioners' sugar
- Juice of ½ lemon
- 2 teaspoon vanilla extract
- ¼ cup plus 2 tablespoons milk

Make the Buns: 1. Brush the insert of a 5- to 6-quart crock pot with butter. Line bottom with parchment paper and brush paper with butter. 2. Combine the warm water, yeast, and honey in a bowl; let stand until foamy, about 5 minutes. Add flour and salt. With an electric mixer on low, mix until just combined. Increase speed to medium and mix for 5 minutes; let stand 10 minutes. Combine butter, both sugars, and cinnamon in a bowl; mix until smooth. 3. Preheat the crock pot. Turn dough out onto a lightly floured work surface and roll into a rectangle, about 9 by 15 inches. Sprinkle dough evenly with cinnamon-sugar mixture. Starting from one long side, roll into a log, pinching seams to seal in filling. Slice log into 10 to 12 rounds, each about 1½ inches thick. 4. Arrange rolls, cut side down, in the cooker. Wrap lid tightly with a clean kitchen towel, gathering ends at top (to absorb condensation). Cover and cook on high until cooked through, 1½ hours (we prefer to bake these on high). After 1 hour, rotate cooker insert to prevent scorching. Turn out onto a wire rack to cool before serving. Make the Glaze: 5. With an electric mixer, whisk confectioners' sugar, lemon juice, and vanilla until smooth. Slowly add ¼ cup milk and beat on medium. Add more milk, a drop at a time up to 2 tablespoons, to reach desired consistency. Drizzle rolls with glaze just before serving.

Crock Pot Frittata Provencal

Prep time: 30 minutes | Cook time: 3 hours | Serves 6

- ½ cup water
- 1 tablespoon olive oil
- 1 medium Yukon Gold potato, peeled and sliced
- 1 small onion, thinly sliced
- ½ teaspoon smoked paprika
- 12 eggs
- 1 teaspoon minced fresh thyme or ¼ teaspoon dried thyme
- 1 teaspoon hot pepper sauce
- ½ teaspoon salt
- ¼ teaspoon pepper
- 1 (4-ounce / 113-g) log fresh goat cheese, coarsely crumbled, divided
- ½ cup chopped soft sun-dried tomatoes (not packed in oil)

1. Layer two 24-inch pieces of aluminum foil; starting with a long side, fold up foil to create a 1-inch wide strip. Shape strip into a coil to make a rack for bottom of a 6-quart oval crock pot. Add water to crock pot; set foil rack in water. 2. In a large skillet, heat oil over medium-high heat. Add potato and onion; cook and stir 5 to 7 minutes or until potato is lightly browned. Stir in paprika. Transfer to a greased 1½-quart baking dish (dish must fit in crock pot). 3. In a large bowl, whisk eggs, thyme, pepper sauce, salt and pepper; stir in 2 ounces (57 g) cheese. Pour over potato mixture. Top with tomatoes and remaining goat cheese. Place dish on foil rack. 4. Cook, covered, on low 3 hours or until eggs are set and a knife inserted near the center comes out clean.

Overnight Oatmeal

Prep time: 5 minutes | Cook time: 3 to 10 hours | Serves 8

- 3¾ cups old-fashioned rolled oats
- 8 cups water
- ½ teaspoon salt
- 4 tablespoons (½ stick) unsalted butter, cut into
- small pieces
- 2 cups milk or cream, warmed, for serving
- ¼ cup cinnamon sugar for serving

1. Coat the insert of a 5- to 7-quart crock pot with nonstick cooking spray or line the insert with a slow-cooker liner according to manufacturer's directions. 2. Combine the oatmeal, water, and salt in the cooker. Cover and cook on low for 8 to 10 hours or on high for 3 to 4 hours, until the oats are creamy. Stir in the butter. Serve with warmed milk and cinnamon sugar.

Nutty "Oatmeal"

Prep time: 10 minutes | Cook time: 8 hours | Serves 6

- 1 tablespoon coconut oil
- 1 cup coconut milk
- 1 cup unsweetened shredded coconut
- ½ cup chopped pecans
- ½ cup sliced almonds
- ¼ cup granulated erythritol
- 1 avocado, diced
- 2 ounces (57 g) protein powder
- 1 teaspoon ground cinnamon
- ¼ teaspoon ground nutmeg
- ½ cup blueberries, for garnish

1. Lightly grease the insert of a slower cooker with the coconut oil. 2. Place the coconut milk, shredded coconut, pecans, almonds, erythritol, avocado, protein powder, cinnamon, and nutmeg in the crock pot. 3. Cover and cook on low for 8 hours. 4. Stir the mixture to create the desired texture. 5. Serve topped with the blueberries.

Breakfast Oatmeal

Prep time: 5 minutes | Cook time: 8 hours | Serves 6

- 2 cups dry rolled oats
- 4 cups water
- 1 teaspoon salt
- ½ to 1 cup chopped dates,
- or raisins, or cranberries, or a mixture of any of these fruits

1. Combine all ingredients in crock pot. 2. Cover and cook on low overnight, or for 8 hours.

Pumpkin-Nutmeg Pudding

Prep time: 15 minutes | Cook time: 6 to 7 hours | Serves 8

- ¼ cup melted butter, divided
- 2½ cups canned pumpkin purée
- 2 cups coconut milk
- 4 eggs
- 1 tablespoon pure vanilla extract
- 1 cup almond flour
- ½ cup granulated erythritol
- 2 ounces (57 g) protein powder
- 1 teaspoon baking powder
- 1 teaspoon ground cinnamon
- ¼ teaspoon ground nutmeg
- Pinch ground cloves

1. Lightly grease the insert of the crock pot with 1 tablespoon of the butter. 2. In a large bowl, whisk together the remaining butter, pumpkin, coconut milk, eggs, and vanilla until well blended. 3. In a small bowl, stir together the almond flour, erythritol, protein powder, baking powder, cinnamon, nutmeg, and cloves. 4. Add the dry ingredients to the wet ingredients and stir to combine. 5. Pour the mixture into the insert. 6. Cover and cook on low for 6 to 7 hours. 7. Serve warm.

Hot Wheat Berry Cereal

Prep time: 5 minutes | Cook time: 10 hours | Serves 4

- 1 cup wheat berries
- 5 cups water

1. Rinse and sort berries. Cover with water and soak all day (or 8 hours) in crock pot. 2. Cover. Cook on low overnight (or 10 hours). 3. Drain, if needed. Serve.

Overnight Apple Oatmeal

Prep time: 10 minutes | Cook time: 6 to 8 hours | Serves 4

- 2 cups skim or 2% milk
- 2 tablespoons honey, or ¼ cup brown sugar
- 1 tablespoon margarine
- ¼ teaspoon salt
- ½ teaspoon ground
- cinnamon
- 1 cup dry rolled oats
- 1 cup apples, chopped
- ½ cup raisins (optional)
- ¼ cup walnuts, chopped
- ½ cup fat-free half-and-half

1. Spray inside of crock pot with nonfat cooking spray. 2. In a mixing bowl, combine all ingredients except half-and-half. Pour into cooker. 3. Cover and cook on low overnight, ideally 6 to 8 hours. The oatmeal is ready to eat in the morning. 4. Stir in the half-and-half just before serving.

Sausage Breakfast Risotto

Prep time: 20 minutes | Cook time: 7 hours | Serves 2

- 8 ounces (227 g) pork sausage
- 1 onion, chopped
- 2 garlic cloves, minced
- Nonstick cooking spray
- 1 cup sliced cremini mushrooms
- 1 cup Arborio rice
- 3 cups chicken stock
- ½ cup milk
- ½ teaspoon salt
- ½ teaspoon dried marjoram leaves
- ⅛ teaspoon freshly ground black pepper
- ⅓ cup grated Parmesan cheese
- 1 tablespoon butter

1. In a medium saucepan over medium heat, cook the sausage, onion, and garlic until the sausage is browned, about 10 minutes, stirring to break up the meat. Drain well. 2. Spray the crock pot with the nonstick cooking spray. 3. In the crock pot, combine the sausage mixture, mushrooms, and rice. Add the stock, milk, salt, marjoram, and pepper, and stir. 4. Cover and cook on low for 7 hours. 5. Stir in the cheese and butter. Let stand for 5 minutes, and then serve.

Overnight Steel-Cut Oats

Prep time: 5 minutes | Cook time: 8 hours | Serves 4 to 5

- 1 cup dry steel-cut oats
- 4 cups water

1. Combine ingredients in crock pot. 2. Cover and cook on low overnight, or for 8 hours. 3. Stir before serving. Serve with your other favorite toppings.

Breakfast Sausage

Prep time: 10 minutes | Cook time: 3 hours | Serves 8

- 1 tablespoon extra-virgin olive oil
- 2 pounds (907 g) ground pork
- 2 eggs
- 1 sweet onion, chopped
- ½ cup almond flour
- 2 teaspoons minced garlic
- 2 teaspoons dried oregano
- 1 teaspoon dried thyme
- 1 teaspoon fennel seeds
- 1 teaspoon freshly ground black pepper
- ½ teaspoon salt

1. Lightly grease the insert of the crock pot with the olive oil. 2. In a large bowl, stir together the pork, eggs, onion, almond flour, garlic, oregano, thyme, fennel seeds, pepper, and salt until well mixed. 3. Transfer the meat mixture to the crock pot's insert and shape it into a loaf, leaving about ½ inch between the sides and meat. 4. Cover, and if your crock pot has a temperature probe, insert it. 5. Cook on low until it reaches an internal temperature of 150ºF (66ºC), about 3 hours. 6. Slice in any way you prefer and serve.

Buttery Coconut Bread

Prep time: 10 minutes | Cook time: 3 to 4 hours | Makes 8 slices

- 1 tablespoon butter, softened
- 6 large eggs
- ½ cup coconut oil, melted
- 1 teaspoon pure vanilla extract
- ¼ teaspoon liquid stevia
- 1 cup almond flour
- ½ cup coconut flour
- 1 ounce (28 g) protein powder
- 1 teaspoon baking powder

1. Grease an 8-by-4-inch loaf pan with the butter. 2. In a medium bowl, whisk together the eggs, oil, vanilla, and stevia until well blended. 3. In a small bowl, stir together the almond flour, coconut flour, protein powder, and baking powder until mixed. 4. Add the dry ingredients to the wet ingredients and stir to combine. 5. Spoon the batter into the loaf pan and place the loaf pan on a rack in the crock pot. 6. Cover and cook on low for 3 to 4 hours, until a knife inserted in the center comes out clean. 7. Cool the bread in the loaf pan for 15 minutes. Then remove the bread from the pan and place onto a wire rack to cool completely. 8. Store in a sealed container in the refrigerator for up to 1 week.

Huevos Rancheros

Prep time: 10 minutes | Cook time: 3 hours | Serves 8

- 1 tablespoon extra-virgin olive oil
- 10 eggs
- 1 cup heavy (whipping) cream
- 1 cup shredded Monterey Jack cheese, divided
- 1 cup prepared or homemade salsa
- 1 scallion, green and white parts, chopped
- 1 jalapeño pepper, chopped
- ½ teaspoon chili powder
- ½ teaspoon salt
- 1 avocado, chopped, for garnish
- 1 tablespoon chopped cilantro, for garnish

1. Lightly grease the insert of the crock pot with the olive oil. 2. In a large bowl, whisk together the eggs, heavy cream, ½ cup of the cheese, salsa, scallion, jalapeño, chili powder, and salt. Pour the mixture into the insert and sprinkle the top with the remaining ½ cup of cheese. 3. Cover and cook until the eggs are firm, about 3 hours on low. 4. Let the eggs cool slightly, then cut into wedges and serve garnished with avocado and cilantro.

Basic Strata

Prep time: 10 minutes | Cook time: 4½ hours | Serves 8 to 10

- 8 cups torn or cubed (1-inch) stale bread, tough crusts removed
- 3½ to 4 cups shredded cheese
- 10 large eggs
- 3 cups milk
- 1½ teaspoons salt
- ½ teaspoon hot sauce

1. Coat the insert of a 5- to 7-quart crock pot with nonstick cooking spray or line it with a slow-cooker liner according to the manufacturer's directions. 2. Spread a layer of the bread into the crock pot and sprinkle with some of the cheese. Continue layering the bread and cheese until it has all been used, saving some cheese for the top. 3. Whisk together the eggs, milk, salt, and hot sauce in a large bowl. Pour the mixture over the cheese and bread and push it down to make sure the bread becomes saturated. Sprinkle the remaining cheese over the top. 4. Cover and cook on low for 4 hours, until the strata is cooked through (170ºF / 77ºC on an instant-read thermometer). Remove the lid and cook for an additional 30 minutes. 5. Serve the strata from the cooker set on warm.

Sausage and Hash-Brown Casserole

Prep time: 25 minutes | Cook time: 2½ to 3 hours | Serves 8

- 1½ pounds (680 g) bulk pork sausage
- 2 medium onions, finely chopped
- 1 Anaheim chile, cored, seeded and finely chopped
- 1 medium red bell pepper, seeded and finely chopped
- 1 teaspoon ground cumin
- ½ teaspoon dried oregano
- 1 (16-ounce / 454-g) package frozen shredded hash brown potatoes,
- defrosted, or 2 cups fresh shredded hash browns
- 6 large eggs, beaten
- 1 cup milk
- 1 cup mayonnaise
- 1 cup prepared salsa (your choice of heat)
- 2 cups shredded mild Cheddar cheese, or 1 cup shredded mild Cheddar mixed with 1 cup shredded Pepper Jack cheese

1. Coat the insert of a 5- to 7-quart crock pot with nonstick cooking spray or line the insert with a slow-cooker liner according the manufacturer's directions. 2. Cook the sausage in a large skillet over high heat until it is no longer pink, breaking up any large pieces with the side of a spoon. 3. Remove all but 1 tablespoon of fat from the pan and heat over medium-high heat. Add the onions, chile, bell pepper, cumin, and oregano and sauté until the onions are softened and translucent, 5 to 6 minutes. Transfer the mixture to a bowl and allow to cool. 4. Add the potatoes to the bowl and stir to blend. In a smaller bowl, whisk together the eggs, milk, and mayonnaise. Pour over the sausage and potato mixture and stir to combine. 5. Transfer half the mixture to the slow-cooker insert, then cover with half the salsa and half the cheese. Repeat the layers with the remaining ingredients. Cover and cook on high for 2½ to 3 hours, until the casserole is puffed, and cooked through (170ºF / 77ºC on an instant-read thermometer). Remove the cover and allow the frittata to rest for 30 minutes. 6. Serve from the cooker set on warm.

Enchiladas Verde

Prep time: 20 minutes | Cook time: 4 to 5 hours | Serves 6 to 8

- 2 tablespoons vegetable oil
- 1 medium onion, finely chopped
- 1 Anaheim chile pepper, seeded and finely chopped
- 4 tablespoons finely chopped fresh cilantro
- 3 cups tomatillo salsa
- ½ cup chicken broth
- 2½ cups finely shredded
- mild Cheddar cheese
- 2 cups finely shredded Monterey Jack or Pepper Jack cheese
- 2 cups crumbled queso fresco
- 2 cups sour cream
- 12 (6-inch) round white or yellow corn tortillas, cut in strips or roughly torn

1. Coat the insert of a 5- to 7-quart crock pot with nonstick cooking spray or line it with a slow-cooker liner according to the manufacturer's directions. 2. Heat the oil in a medium saucepan over medium-high heat. Add the onion and chile and sauté until they are softened and fragrant, 3 to 5 minutes. 3. Add 2 tablespoons of the cilantro, the salsa, and broth and simmer for 30 minutes, until the sauce is reduced and thickened a bit. Remove from the heat and set aside to cool slightly. Put the Cheddar and Monterey Jack cheese in a mixing bowl and stir to combine. 4. Put the queso fresco, the remaining 2 tablespoons cilantro, and the sour cream in another bowl and stir to combine. Spoon a thin layer of the sauce on the bottom of the crock pot insert. Layer one-third of the tortillas evenly on the bottom of the crock pot. 5. Spread half the queso fresco mixture over the tortillas and top with one-third of the shredded cheese. Repeat, layering the tortillas, sauce, queso fresco, and shredded cheese. Finish layering the remaining tortillas, sauce, and shredded cheese. Cover and cook on low for 3 to 4 hours, until the casserole is cooked through and the cheese is bubbling. Remove the cover and cook for an additional 30 to 45 minutes. 6. Serve from the cooker set on warm.

Veggie Hash with Eggs

Prep time: 20 minutes | Cook time: 6¼ hours | Serves 2

- Nonstick cooking spray
- 1 onion, chopped
- 2 garlic cloves, minced
- 1 red bell pepper, chopped
- 1 yellow summer squash, chopped
- 2 carrots, chopped
- 2 Yukon Gold potatoes, peeled and chopped
- 2 large tomatoes, seeded and chopped
- ¼ cup vegetable broth
- ½ teaspoon salt
- ⅛ teaspoon freshly ground black pepper
- ½ teaspoon dried thyme leaves
- 3 or 4 eggs
- ½ teaspoon ground sweet paprika

1. Spray the crock pot with the nonstick cooking spray. 2. In the crock pot, combine all the ingredients except the eggs and paprika, and stir. 3. Cover and cook on low for 6 hours. 4. Uncover and make 1 indentation in the vegetable mixture for each egg. Break 1 egg into a small cup and slip the egg into an indentation. Repeat with the remaining eggs. Sprinkle with the paprika. 5. Cover and cook on low for 10 to 15 minutes, or until the eggs are just set, and serve.

Summer Squash and Mushroom Strata

Prep time: 20 minutes | Cook time: 6 hours | Serves 2

- 1 onion, chopped
- 2 garlic cloves, minced
- 1½ cups sliced cremini mushrooms
- 1 red bell pepper, chopped
- 1 yellow summer squash, chopped
- Nonstick cooking spray
- 6 slices French bread, cubed
- 1 cup shredded Cheddar
- cheese
- 1 cup shredded Swiss cheese
- 5 eggs, beaten
- 1 cup milk
- 1 tablespoon Dijon mustard
- ½ teaspoon salt
- ½ teaspoon dried basil leaves
- ⅛ teaspoon freshly ground black pepper

1. In a medium bowl, mix the onion, garlic, mushrooms, bell pepper, and squash. 2. Spray the crock pot with the nonstick cooking spray. 3. In the crock pot, layer the bread, vegetable mixture, and Cheddar and Swiss cheeses. 4. In a medium bowl, beat the eggs, milk, mustard, salt, basil, and pepper until combined. 5. Pour the egg mixture into the crock pot. 6. Cover and cook on low for 6 hours, or until the temperature registers 160ºF (71ºC) on a food thermometer. 7. Cut into squares and serve.

Three-Cheese Vegetable Strata

Prep time: 20 minutes | Cook time: 6 hours | Serves 2

- 1 tablespoon extra-virgin olive oil
- 1 tablespoon butter
- 1 onion, chopped
- 2 garlic cloves, minced
- 1½ cups baby spinach leaves
- 1 red bell pepper, chopped
- 1 large tomato, seeded and chopped
- 1 cup cubed ham
- Nonstick cooking spray
- 5 eggs, beaten
- 1 cup milk
- ½ teaspoon salt
- ½ teaspoon dried thyme leaves
- ⅛ teaspoon freshly ground black pepper
- 6 slices French bread, cubed
- 1 cup shredded Cheddar cheese
- ½ cup shredded Swiss cheese
- ¼ cup grated Parmesan cheese

1. In a medium saucepan over medium heat, heat the olive oil and butter. Add the onion and garlic, and sauté, stirring, until tender, about 6 minutes. 2. Add the spinach and cook until wilted, about 5 minutes. Remove from the heat and add the bell pepper, tomato, and ham. 3. Line the crock pot with heavy-duty foil and spray with the nonstick cooking spray. 4. In a medium bowl, beat the eggs, milk, salt, thyme, and black pepper well. 5. In the crock pot, layer half of the French bread. Top with half of the vegetable and ham mixture, and sprinkle with half of the Cheddar and Swiss cheeses. Repeat the layers. 6. Pour the egg mixture over everything, and sprinkle with the Parmesan cheese. 7. Cover and cook on low for 6 hours, or until the temperature registers 160ºF (71ºC) on a food thermometer and the mixture is set. 8. Using the foil sling, remove from the crock pot, and serve.

Breakfast Wassail

Prep time: 5 minutes | Cook time: 3 hours | Makes 4 quarts

- 1 (64-ounce / 1.8-kg) bottle cranberry juice
- 1 (32-ounce / 907-g) bottle apple juice
- 1 (12-ounce / 340-g) can frozen pineapple juice
- concentrate
- 1 (12-ounce / 340-g) can frozen lemonade concentrate
- 3 to 4 cinnamon sticks
- 1 quart water (optional)

1. Combine all ingredients except water in crock pot. Add water if mixture is too sweet. 2. Cover. Cook on low 3 hours.

Crock Pot Oatmeal

Prep time: 15 minutes | Cook time: 8 to 9 hours | Serves 7 to 8

- 2 cups dry rolled oats
- 4 cups water
- 1 large apple, peeled and chopped
- 1 cup raisins
- 1 teaspoon cinnamon
- 1 to 2 tablespoons orange zest

1. Combine all ingredients in your crock pot. 2. Cover and cook on low 8 to 9 hours. 3. Serve topped with brown sugar, if you wish, and milk.

Keto Granola

Prep time: 10 minutes | Cook time: 3 to 4 hours | Serves 16

- ½ cup coconut oil, melted
- 2 teaspoons pure vanilla extract
- 1 teaspoon maple extract
- 1 cup chopped pecans
- 1 cup sunflower seeds
- 1 cup unsweetened
- shredded coconut
- ½ cup hazelnuts
- ½ cup slivered almonds
- ¼ cup granulated erythritol
- ½ teaspoon cinnamon
- ¼ teaspoon ground nutmeg
- ¼ teaspoon salt

1. Lightly grease the insert of the crock pot with 1 tablespoon of the coconut oil. 2. In a large bowl, whisk together the remaining coconut oil, vanilla, and maple extract. Add the pecans, sunflower seeds, coconut, hazelnuts, almonds, erythritol, cinnamon, nutmeg, and salt. Toss to coat the nuts and seeds. 3. Transfer the mixture to the insert. 4. Cover and cook on low for 3 to 4 hours, until the granola is crispy. 5. Transfer the granola to a baking sheet covered in parchment or foil to cool. 6. Store in a sealed container in the refrigerator for up to 2 weeks.

Polenta

Prep time: 10 minutes | Cook time:2 to 9 hours | Serves 8 to 10

- 4 tablespoons melted butter, divided
- ¼ teaspoon paprika
- 6 cups boiling water
- 2 cups dry cornmeal
- 2 teaspoons salt

1. Use 1 tablespoon butter to lightly grease the inside of the crock pot. Sprinkle in paprika. Turn to high setting. 2. Add remaining ingredients to crock pot in the order listed, including 1 tablespoon butter. Stir well. 3. Cover and cook on high 2 to 3 hours, or on low 6 to 9 hours. Stir occasionally. 4. Pour hot cooked polenta into 2 lightly greased loaf pans. Chill 8 hours or overnight. 5. To serve, cut into ¼-inch-thick slices. Melt 2 tablespoons butter in large nonstick skillet, then lay in slices and cook until browned. Turn to brown other side. 6. For breakfast, serve with your choice of sweetener.

Dill-Asparagus Bake

Prep time: 10 minutes | Cook time: 4 to 5 hours | Serves 8

- 1 tablespoon extra-virgin olive oil
- 10 eggs
- ¾ cup coconut milk
- ½ teaspoon salt
- ¼ teaspoon freshly ground black pepper
- 2 teaspoons chopped fresh dill
- 2 cups chopped asparagus spears
- 1 cup chopped cooked bacon

1. Lightly grease the insert of the crock pot with the olive oil. 2. In a medium bowl, whisk together the eggs, coconut milk, salt, pepper, and dill. Stir in the asparagus and bacon. Pour the mixture into the crock pot. 3. Cover and cook on low for 4 to 5 hours. 4. Serve warm.

Blueberry Apple Waffle Topping

Prep time: 10 minutes | Cook time: 3 hours | Serves 10 to 12

- 1 quart natural applesauce, unsweetened
- 2 Granny Smith apples, unpeeled, cored, and sliced
- 1 pint fresh or frozen blueberries
- ½ tablespoon ground
- cinnamon
- ½ cup pure maple syrup
- 1 teaspoon almond flavoring
- ½ cup walnuts, chopped
- Nonfat cooking spray

1. Stir together applesauce, apples, and blueberries in crock pot sprayed with nonfat cooking spray. 2. Add cinnamon and maple syrup. 3. Cover. Cook on low 3 hours. 4. Add almond flavoring and walnuts just before serving.

Chapter ②

Beans and Grains

Farro Pilaf

Prep time: 10 minutes | Cook time: 6 hours | Serves 2

- 1 cup farro, rinsed
- 1 onion, chopped
- 1 cup sliced shiitake mushrooms
- 1 leek, white part only, chopped
- 3 garlic cloves, minced
- 2½ cups vegetable broth
- 1 teaspoon dried marjoram leaves
- ½ teaspoon salt
- ⅛ teaspoon freshly ground black pepper
- 2 tablespoons butter

1. In the crock pot, combine all the ingredients except the butter, and stir. 2. Cover and cook on low for 6 hours, or until the farro is tender. 3. Stir in the butter and serve.

Beans with Chicken Sausage and Escarole

Prep time: 15 minutes | Cook time: 4 hours | Serves 6

- 12 ounces (340 g) chicken sausage, cut into ¼-inch rounds
- 1 (15-ounce / 425-g) can cannellini beans, drained and rinsed
- 1 (15-ounce / 425-g) can chickpeas, drained and rinsed
- 1 (28-ounce / 794-g) can whole tomatoes, drained and chopped
- 1½ cups chicken stock
- 1 bay leaf
- 1 teaspoon dried thyme
- ¼ teaspoon red pepper flakes
- ½ teaspoon sea salt
- ¼ teaspoon black pepper
- 1 small head escarole, chopped
- ¼ cup coarsely grated Parmigiano-Reggiano cheese
- 2 tablespoons chopped fresh flat-leaf parsley

1. Combine sausage, cannellini beans, chickpeas, tomatoes, and stock in the crock pot. Sprinkle on the bay leaf, thyme, red pepper flakes, ½ teaspoon salt, and ¼ teaspoon pepper. 2. Cover and cook on low for 4 hours. 3. Stir in the escarole and cook an additional 5 to 8 minutes, until just wilted. Stir in the Parmigiano-Reggiano and parsley. Season with additional sea salt and black pepper. Serve hot.

Crock Pot Vegetarian Chili

Prep time: 15 minutes | Cook time: 4 to 8 hours | Serves 4

- 1 (28-ounce / 794-g) can chopped whole tomatoes, with the juice
- 1 medium green bell pepper, chopped
- 1 (15-ounce / 425-g) can
- red beans, drained and rinsed
- 1 (15-ounce / 425-g) can black beans, drained and rinsed
- 1 yellow onion, chopped
- 1 tablespoon olive oil
- 1 tablespoon onion powder
- 1 teaspoon garlic powder
- 1 teaspoon cayenne pepper
- 1 teaspoon paprika
- ½ teaspoon sea salt
- ½ teaspoon black pepper
- 1 large Hass avocado, pitted, peeled, and chopped, for garnish

1. Combine the tomatoes, bell pepper, red beans, black beans, and onion in the crock pot. Sprinkle with the onion powder, garlic powder, cayenne pepper, paprika, ½ teaspoon salt, and ½ teaspoon black pepper. 2. Cover and cook on high for 4 to 6 hours or on low for 8 hours, or until thick. 3. Season with salt and black pepper if needed. Served hot, garnished with some of the avocado.

Pineapple Baked Beans

Prep time: 15 minutes | Cook time: 4 to 8 hours | Serves 6 to 8

- 1 pound (454 g) ground beef
- 1 (28-ounce / 794-g) can baked beans
- 1 (8-ounce / 227-g) can pineapple tidbits, drained
- 1 (4½-ounce / 128-g) can sliced mushrooms, drained
- 1 large onion, chopped
- 1 large green pepper, chopped
- ½ cup barbecue sauce
- 2 tablespoons soy sauce
- 1 clove garlic, minced
- ½ teaspoon salt
- ¼ teaspoon pepper

1. Brown ground beef in skillet. Drain. Place in crock pot. 2. Stir in remaining ingredients. Mix well. 3. Cover Cook on low 4 to 8 hours, or until bubbly. Serve.

Wild Rice

Prep time: 10 minutes | Cook time: 2½ to 3 hours | Serves 5

- 1 cup wild rice or wild rice mixture, uncooked
- ½ cup sliced fresh mushrooms
- ½ cup diced onions
- ½ cup diced green or red
- bell peppers
- 1 tablespoon oil
- ½ teaspoon salt
- ¼ teaspoon black pepper
- 2½ cups fat-free, low-sodium chicken broth

1. Layer rice and vegetables in crock pot. Pour oil, salt, and pepper over vegetables. Stir. 2. Heat chicken broth. Pour over all ingredients in crock pot. 3. Cover. Cook on high 2½ to 3 hours, or until rice is soft and liquid is absorbed.

White Beans with Kale

Prep time: 15 minutes | Cook time: 7½ hours | Serves 2

- 1 onion, chopped
- 1 leek, white part only, sliced
- 2 celery stalks, sliced
- 2 garlic cloves, minced
- 1 cup dried white lima beans or cannellini beans, sorted and rinsed
- 2 cups vegetable broth
- ½ teaspoon salt
- ½ teaspoon dried thyme leaves
- ⅛ teaspoon freshly ground black pepper
- 3 cups torn kale

1. In the crock pot, combine all the ingredients except the kale. 2. Cover and cook on low for 7 hours, or until the beans are tender. 3. Add the kale and stir. 4. Cover and cook on high for 30 minutes, or until the kale is tender but still firm, and serve.

Borlotti Beans with Spiced Polenta Dumplings

Prep time: 30 minutes | Cook time: 5 to 9 hours | Serves 8

- Beans:
- 1 pound (454 g) dry borlotti beans
- 6 cups chicken stock
- 1 medium yellow onion, chopped
- 1 medium red bell pepper, diced
- 2 stalks celery, sliced
- 1 cup corn kernels
- 2 cloves garlic, minced
- 1 tablespoon paprika
- 1 tablespoon red pepper flakes
- 1 teaspoon dried rosemary
- 1 teaspoon dried thyme
- 2 tablespoons red wine vinegar
- Sea salt
- Polenta Dumplings:
- ½ cup all-purpose flour
- ½ cup cornmeal
- ½ teaspoon baking powder
- ¼ teaspoon sea salt
- 2 tablespoons cold butter, cut into cubes
- 1 fresh peperoncino, seeded and minced
- Zest of 1 lime
- ½ cup buttermilk
- ½ cup fresh flat-leaf parsley, chopped, for serving
- ½ cup sliced black olives, for serving

Make the Beans: 1. Combine the beans, stock, onion, bell pepper, celery, corn, and garlic in the crock pot. Sprinkle with the paprika, red pepper flakes, rosemary, and thyme. 2. Cover and cook on high for 4 hours or on low for 8 hours. Make the Dumplings: 3. At 30 minutes before the end of the cooking time, whisk together the flour, cornmeal, baking powder, and ¼ teaspoon salt in a medium bowl. 4. Add the butter and use a pastry cutter or a fork to cut the butter into the flour mixture until the mixture resembles coarse meal. Add the peperoncino and lime zest and toss to coat. Add the buttermilk and stir to form a dough. 5. After the beans are fully cooked, stir in the red wine vinegar and 1½ teaspoons sea salt. Using generous tablespoonfuls of dough, drop 8 dumplings on top of the stew. 6. Cover and cook on high for 1 hour. 7. Serve each portion of stew topped with a dumpling. Serve hot with parsley and olives sprinkled on top.

Colonial Williamsburg Spoon Bread

Prep time: 10 minutes | Cook time: 3½ hours | Serves 8

- 3 cups cornmeal
- 3 cups water
- 3 cups milk
- ⅓ cup sugar
- 2 tablespoons baking powder
- ½ cup (1 stick) unsalted butter, melted and cooled slightly
- 8 large eggs

1. Coat the insert of a 5- to 7-quart crock pot with nonstick cooking spray. 2. Put the cornmeal, water and milk in a large mixing bowl and stir for 3 to 5 minutes. (This will ensure a light spoon bread). Add the sugar, baking powder, butter, and eggs and beat with a wooden spoon until the mixture is smooth. transfer the mixture to the slow-cooker insert. 3. Cover and cook on high for 3 hours, until the top is set. Uncover and cook for an additional 30 minutes. 4. Serve the spoon bread from the cooker set on warm.

Spicy Black Beans with Root Veggies

Prep time: 20 minutes | Cook time: 8 hours | Serves 2

- 1 onion, chopped
- 1 leek, white part only, sliced
- 3 garlic cloves, minced
- 1 jalapeño pepper, minced
- 2 Yukon Gold potatoes, peeled and cubed
- 1 parsnip, peeled and cubed
- 1 carrot, sliced
- 1 cup dried black beans, sorted and rinsed
- 2 cups vegetable broth
- 2 teaspoons chili powder
- ½ teaspoon dried marjoram leaves
- ½ teaspoon salt
- ⅛ teaspoon freshly ground black pepper
- ⅛ teaspoon crushed red pepper flakes

1. In the crock pot, combine all the ingredients. 2. Cover and cook on low for 7 to 8 hours, or until the beans and vegetables are tender, and serve.

Butternut Squash Risotto

Prep time: 10 minutes | Cook time: 2½ hours | Serves 4 to 6

- ½ cup (1 stick) unsalted butter
- 2 tablespoons olive oil
- ½ cup finely chopped shallots (about 4 medium)
- 2 cups diced peeled and seeded butternut squash
- 1½ cups Arborio or Carnaroli rice
- ¼ cup dry white wine or vermouth
- 4¼ cups chicken broth
- ½ cup freshly grated Parmigiano-Reggiano cheese

1. Coat the insert of a 5- to 7-quart crock pot with nonstick cooking spray or line it with a slow-cooker liner according to the manufacturer's directions. 2. Heat ¼ cup of the butter with the oil in a large saucepan over medium-high heat. Add the shallots and squash and sauté until the shallots are softened, about 3 minutes. Add the rice and cook, tossing to coat with the butter, until the rice is opaque. Add the wine and cook until the wine evaporates. 3. Transfer the mixture to the slow-cooker insert and stir in the broth. Cover and cook on high for 2½ hours; check the risotto at 2 hours to make sure the broth hasn't evaporated. Stir in the remaining ¼ cup butter and ¼ cup of the cheese. 4. Serve the risotto immediately with the remaining cheese on the side.

Mediterranean Rice and Sausage

Prep time: 10 minutes | Cook time: 2 to 5 hours | Serves 4

- ¼ cup olive oil, plus 1 tablespoon
- 1½ cups uncooked brown rice
- 1 large yellow onion, chopped
- 2 cloves garlic, minced
- ½ green bell pepper, chopped
- ¾ pound (340 g) bulk
- ground Italian sausage
- 4 cups tomato juice
- 1 teaspoon Worcestershire sauce
- ½ cup red wine of your choice
- ½ teaspoon cayenne pepper
- 1 teaspoon sea salt
- ¼ teaspoon black pepper

1. Heat ¼ cup of the olive oil over medium-high heat in a medium skillet. Add the brown rice and brown, tossing frequently, for 2 to 3 minutes. Remove the rice to a small bowl and set aside. 2. In same skillet, heat the remaining 1 tablespoon olive oil over medium-high heat. Add the onion and garlic and sauté for 1 or 2 minutes until fragrant. 3. Add the bell pepper. Cook for 2 or 3 minutes until the bell pepper has softened. Remove the vegetables to a small bowl and set aside. 4. Add the Italian sausage to the skillet. Cook over medium-high heat until just browned, about 4 minutes. Remove from the heat. 5. In a blender or food processor, purée one-half of the vegetable mix, which should now be just cool enough to handle, until just smooth. 6. To the crock pot, add the tomato juice, Worcestershire sauce, red wine, puréed vegetables, and cooked vegetables. Add browned rice. Add the browned Italian sausage. Sprinkle in the cayenne pepper, 1 teaspoon salt, and ¼ teaspoon pepper. 7. Cover and cook on high for 2 hours. Switch to low heat and continue cooking for 5 hours. 8. Season with additional salt and pepper, as needed. Serve hot.

Wild Rice Pilaf

Prep time: 10 minutes | Cook time: 3½ to 5 hours | Serves 6

- 1½ cups wild rice, uncooked
- ½ cup finely chopped onion
- 1 (14-ounce / 397-g) chicken broth
- 2 cups water
- 1 (4-ounce / 113-g) can sliced mushrooms, drained
- ½ teaspoon dried thyme leaves
- Nonstick cooking spray

1. Spray crock pot with nonstick cooking spray. 2. Rinse rice and drain well. 3. Combine rice, onion, chicken broth, and water in crock pot. Mix well. 4. Cover and cook on high 3 to 4 hours. 5. Add mushrooms and thyme and stir gently. 6. Cover and cook on low 30 to 60 minutes longer, or until wild rice pops and is tender.

Mixed crock pot Beans

Prep time: 10 minutes | Cook time: 4 to 5 hours | Serves 6

- 1 (16-ounce / 454-g) can kidney beans, drained
- 1 (15½-ounce / 439-g) can baked beans, undrained
- 1 pint home-frozen, or 1 (1-pound / 454-g) package frozen, lima beans
- 1 pint home-frozen, or 1 (1-pound / 454-g) package
- frozen, green beans
- 4 slices lean turkey bacon, browned and crumbled
- ½ cup ketchup
- ⅓ cup sugar
- ⅓ cup brown sugar
- 2 tablespoons vinegar
- ½ teaspoon salt

1. Combine beans and bacon in crock pot. 2. Stir together remaining ingredients. Add to beans and mix well. 3. Cover. Cook on low 4 to 5 hours.

Saffron Rice

Prep time: 10 minutes | Cook time: 2 hours | Serves 8 to 10

- ½ cup (1 stick) unsalted butter
- ½ cup finely chopped shallots
- About 1 teaspoon saffron threads, crushed in the
- palm of your hand
- 3 cups converted white rice
- 4½ to 5½ cups chicken broth
- 2 cups frozen petite peas, defrosted

1. Spray the insert of a 5- to 7-quart crock pot with nonstick cooking spray or line it with a slow-cooker liner according to the manufacturer's directions. 2. Melt the butter in a small sauté pan over medium-high heat. Add the shallots and saffron and sauté until the shallots are softened, about 3 minutes. Transfer to the slow-cooker insert. 3. Add the rice and 4½ cups of the broth and stir to combine. cover and cook on high for 2 hours, until the rice is tender and the liquid is absorbed. Uncover the cooker and stir in the peas. 4. Serve from the cooker set on warm.

Barbecued Lentils

Prep time: 5 minutes | Cook time: 6 to 8 hours | Serves 8

- 2 cups barbecue sauce
- 3½ cups water
- 1 pound (454 g) dry lentils
- 1 package vegetarian hot dogs, sliced

1. Combine all ingredients in crock pot. 2. Cover. Cook on low 6 to 8 hours.

Risi Bisi (Peas and Rice)

Prep time: 15 minutes | Cook time: 2½ to 3½ hours | Serves 6

- 1½ cups converted long-grain white rice, uncooked
- ¾ cup chopped onions
- 2 garlic cloves, minced
- 2 (14½-ounce / 411-g) cans reduced-sodium chicken broth
- ⅓ cup water
- ¾ teaspoon Italian seasoning
- ½ teaspoon dried basil leaves
- ½ cup frozen baby peas, thawed
- ¼ cup grated Parmesan cheese

1. Combine rice, onions, and garlic in crock pot. 2. In saucepan, mix together chicken broth and water. Bring to boil. Add Italian seasoning and basil leaves. Stir into rice mixture. 3. Cover. Cook on low 2 to 3 hours, or until liquid is absorbed. 4. Stir in peas. Cover. Cook 30 minutes. Stir in cheese.

Risotto alla Milanese

Prep time: 10 minutes | Cook time: 2½ hours | Serves 4 to 6

- ½ cup (1 stick) unsalted butter
- 2 tablespoons olive oil
- 1 teaspoon saffron threads
- ½ cup finely chopped shallots (about 4 medium)
- 1½ cups Arborio or
- Carnaroli rice
- ¼ cup dry white wine or vermouth
- 4 cups chicken broth
- ½ cup freshly grated Parmigiano-Reggiano cheese

1. Coat the insert of a 5- to 7-quart crock pot with nonstick cooking spray or line it with a slow-cooker liner according to the manufacturer's directions. 2. Melt ¼ cup of the butter with the oil in a large saucepan over medium-high heat. Add the saffron and shallots and cook, stirring, until the shallots are softened. Add the rice and cook, coating the rice with the butter, until the rice begins to look opaque. Add the wine and allow it to evaporate. 3. Transfer the contents of the saucepan to the slow-cooker insert. Add the broth and stir to incorporate it. Cover and cook on high for 2½ hours; check the risotto at 2 hours to make sure that the broth hasn't evaporated. At the end of the cooking time, the risotto should be tender and creamy. Stir in the remaining ¼ cup butter and ¼ cup of the cheese. 4. Serve the risotto with the remaining cheese on the side.

Risotto with Gorgonzola

Prep time: 10 minutes | Cook time: 2½ hours | Serves 4 to 6

- ½ cup (1 stick) unsalted butter
- 2 tablespoons olive oil
- ½ cup finely chopped shallots (about 4 medium)
- 1½ cups Arborio or
- Carnaroli rice
- ¼ cup dry white wine or vermouth
- 4 cups chicken broth
- 1 cup crumbled Gorgonzola cheese

1. Coat the insert of a 5- to 7-quart crock pot with nonstick cooking spray or line it with a slow-cooker liner according to the manufacturer's directions. 2. Heat ¼ cup of the butter with the oil in a large saucepan over medium-high heat. Add the shallots and sauté until softened, about 4 minutes. Add the rice and cook, stirring to coat with the butter, until the rice begins to look opaque. Add the wine and cook until the wine evaporates. 3. Transfer the mixture to the slow-cooker insert and stir in the broth. Cover and cook on high for 2½ hours; check the risotto at 2 hours to make sure that the broth hasn't evaporated. 4. Stir in the remaining butter and Gorgonzola before serving immediately.

Arroz con Queso

Prep time: 15 minutes | Cook time: 6 to 9 hours | Serves 6 to 8

- 1 (14½-ounce / 411-g) can whole tomatoes, mashed
- 1 (15-ounce / 425-g) can Mexican style beans, undrained
- 1½ cups long-grain rice, uncooked
- 1 cup shredded Monterey Jack cheese
- 1 large onion, finely chopped
- 1 cup cottage cheese
- 1 (4¼-ounce / 120-g) can chopped green chili peppers, drained
- 1 tablespoon oil
- 3 garlic cloves, minced
- 1 teaspoon salt
- 1 cup shredded Monterey Jack cheese

1. Combine all ingredients except final cup of cheese. Pour into well greased crock pot. 2. Cover. Cook on low 6 to 9 hours. 3. Sprinkle with remaining cheese before serving.

Hometown Spanish Rice

Prep time: 20 minutes | Cook time: 2 to 4 hours | Serves 6 to 8

- 1 large onion, chopped
- 1 bell pepper, chopped
- 1 pound (454 g) bacon, cooked, and broken into bite-size pieces
- 2 cups long-grain rice, cooked
- 1 (28-ounce / 794-g) can stewed tomatoes with juice
- Grated Parmesan cheese (optional)
- Nonstick cooking spray

1. Sauté onion and pepper in a small nonstick frying pan until tender. 2. Spray interior of crock pot with nonstick cooking spray. 3. Combine all ingredients in the crock pot. 4. Cover and cook on low 4 hours, or on high 2 hours, or until heated through. 5. Sprinkle with Parmesan cheese just before serving, if you wish.

Chapter 3

Poultry

Roasted Red Pepper and Mozzarella Stuffed Chicken Breasts

Prep time: 15 minutes | Cook time: 6 to 8 hours | Serves 2

- 1 teaspoon extra-virgin olive oil
- 2 boneless, skinless chicken breasts
- ⅛ teaspoon sea salt
- Freshly ground black pepper
- 2 roasted red bell peppers, cut into thin strips
- 2 ounces (57 g) sliced mozzarella cheese
- ¼ cup roughly chopped fresh basil

1. Grease the inside of the crock pot with the olive oil. 2. Slice the chicken breasts through the center horizontally until nearly sliced in half. Open as if opening a book. Season all sides of the chicken with the salt and pepper. 3. Place a layer of the roasted peppers on one inside half of each chicken breast. Top the peppers with the mozzarella slices. Then sprinkle the cheese with the fresh basil. Fold the other half of the chicken over the filling. 4. Carefully place the stuffed chicken breasts into the crock pot, making sure the filling does not escape. Cover and cook on low for 6 to 8 hours, or until the chicken is cooked through.

Thai Peanut Wings

Prep time: 20 minutes | Cook time: 3 hours | Serves 8

- 3 pounds (1.4 kg) chicken wing drumettes
- ¼ cup olive oil
- 1½ teaspoons salt
- 1 teaspoon sweet paprika
- Freshly ground black pepper
- Sauce:
- 1 (14-ounce / 397-g) can coconut milk
- ½ cup chicken broth
- 1 cup smooth peanut butter
- ¼ cup firmly packed brown sugar
- 2 tablespoons soy sauce
- 2 teaspoons freshly grated ginger
- ¼ teaspoon hot sauce
- ½ cup finely chopped fresh cilantro, for garnish
- ½ cup finely chopped roasted peanuts, for garnish

1. Coat the insert of a 5- to 7-quart crock pot with nonstick cooking spray. Preheat the broiler for 10 minutes. 2. Put the wings, olive oil, salt, paprika, and a generous grinding of pepper in a large mixing bowl and toss until the wings are evenly coated. Arrange the wings on a wire rack in a baking sheet and broil until the wings are crispy on one side, about 5 minutes. 3. Turn the wings and broil until crispy and browned, an additional 5 minutes. 4. Remove the wings from the oven.

If you would like to do this step ahead of time, cool the wings and refrigerate for up to 2 days. Otherwise, put the wings in the prepared cooker insert. 5. Combine all the sauce ingredients in a small saucepan over medium heat and stir. 6. Heat the sauce until it begins to boil. Pour the sauce over the wings and turn to coat. 7. Cover and cook on high for 3 hours, turning the wings several times to coat in the sauce. 8. Garnish the wings with the cilantro and peanuts and serve from the cooker set on warm.

Sweet and Spicy Chicken

Prep time: 10 minutes | Cook time: 3½ hours | Serves 6

- 2 teaspoons ground cumin
- ½ teaspoon ground cinnamon
- ¾ teaspoon coarse sea salt
- ½ teaspoon black pepper
- 4 chicken leg quarters
- 1 tablespoon extra-virgin olive oil
- 1 medium yellow onion, cut into ½-inch wedges
- (root end left intact)
- 3 garlic cloves, minced
- 1 (3-inch) piece fresh peeled ginger, sliced into rounds
- 1 (28-ounce / 794-g) can diced tomatoes, with the juice
- ½ cup raisins

1. In a large resealable plastic bag, combine the cumin, cinnamon, salt, and black pepper. Add the chicken to the bag, reseal, and toss to coat. 2. In a large skillet over medium-high heat, heat the olive oil. Add the chicken, skin-side down, and cook until golden, about 4 minutes. Turn and cook 2 additional minutes. 3. Place the onion, garlic, and ginger in the crock pot. 4. Add the chicken, skin-side up, to crock pot. Top the chicken with the tomatoes and raisins. 5. Cover and cook until chicken is tender, 3½ hours on high or 6 hours on low. Serve hot.

Chicken with Applesauce

Prep time: 20 minutes | Cook time: 2 to 3 hours | Serves 4

- 4 boneless, skinless chicken breast halves
- Salt to taste
- Pepper to taste
- 4 to 5 tablespoons oil
- 2 cups applesauce
- ¼ cup barbecue sauce
- ½ teaspoon poultry seasoning
- 2 teaspoons honey
- ½ teaspoon lemon juice

1. Season chicken with salt and pepper. Brown in oil for 5 minutes per side. 2. Cut up chicken into 1-inch chunks and transfer to crock pot. 3. Combine remaining ingredients. Pour over chicken and mix together well. 4. Cover. Cook on high 2 to 3 hours, or until chicken is tender. 5. Serve.

Turkey Meat Loaf

Prep time: 15 minutes | Cook time: 6 to 8 hours | Serves 8

- 1½ pounds (680 g) lean ground turkey
- 2 egg whites
- ⅓ cup ketchup
- 1 tablespoon Worcestershire sauce
- 1 teaspoon dried basil
- ½ teaspoon salt
- ½ teaspoon black pepper
- 2 small onions, chopped
- 2 potatoes, finely shredded
- 2 small red bell peppers, finely chopped

1. Combine all ingredients in a large bowl. 2. Shape into a loaf to fit in your crock pot. Place in crock pot. 3. Cover. Cook on low 6 to 8 hours.

Scalloped Chicken with Stuffing

Prep time: 10 minutes | Cook time: 2 to 3 hours | Serves 4 to 6

- 4 cups cooked chicken
- 1 box stuffing mix for chicken
- 2 eggs
- 1 cup water
- 1½ cups milk
- 1 cup frozen peas

1. Combine chicken and dry stuffing mix. Place in crock pot. 2. Beat eggs, water, and milk together in a bowl. Pour over chicken and stuffing. 3. Cover. Cook on high 2 to 3 hours. 4. Add frozen peas during last hour of cooking.

Pheasant with Mushrooms and Olives

Prep time: 15 minutes | Cook time: 4 to 7 hours | Serves 6

- 2 tablespoons olive oil
- ¾ cup all-purpose flour
- 1 teaspoon sea salt
- ¼ teaspoon black pepper
- 2 pheasants, rinsed, patted dry, and cut into bite-size pieces
- 1 yellow onion, sliced and separated into rings
- 1 cup cremini mushrooms, sliced
- 3 cloves garlic, minced
- 1 cup dry white wine
- 1 cup chicken stock
- ½ cup sliced black olives

1. Place the flour, salt, and pepper into a resealable plastic bag, and shake to combine. 2. Place the pheasant pieces into the bag with the flour mixture, and shake until evenly coated. 3. Heat the olive oil in a large skillet over medium-high heat. 4. Shake any excess flour off of the pheasant pieces, and place them in the hot oil. Cook until the pheasant is brown on both sides, about 6 minutes. 5. Place the pheasant into the crock pot, reserving the oil in the skillet. 6. Add the onion and cook in the remaining oil in the skillet until it softens, about 3 minutes. 7. Stir the mushrooms and garlic into the oil and onion, and continue cooking and stirring until the mushrooms have softened and the garlic has mellowed, about 5 minutes more. 8. Pour the wine into the skillet and bring to a boil. Boil for 5 minutes; then pour in the chicken stock and return to a boil. 9. Pour the mushroom mixture into the crock pot, and sprinkle with the sliced black olives. 10. Cover and cook on high for 4 hours or on low for 7 hours. Serve hot.

Orange Chicken and Sweet Potatoes

Prep time: 10 minutes | Cook time: 3 to 10 hours | Serves 6

- 2 to 3 sweet potatoes, peeled and sliced
- 3 whole chicken breasts, halved
- ⅔ cup flour plus 3 tablespoons, divided
- 1 teaspoon salt
- 1 teaspoon nutmeg
- ½ teaspoon cinnamon
- Dash pepper
- Dash garlic powder
- 1 (10¾-ounce / 305-g) can cream of celery or cream of chicken soup
- 1 (4-ounce / 113-g) can sliced mushrooms, drained
- ½ cup orange juice
- ½ teaspoon grated orange rind
- 2 teaspoons brown sugar

1. Place sweet potatoes in bottom of crock pot. 2. Rinse chicken breasts and pat dry. Combine ⅔ cup flour, salt, nutmeg, cinnamon, pepper, and garlic powder. Thoroughly coat chicken in flour mixture. Place on top of sweet potatoes. 3. Combine soup with remaining ingredients. Stir well. Pour over chicken breasts. 4. Cover. Cook on low 8 to 10 hours, or on high 3 to 4 hours. 5. Serve.

Chicken and Rice

Prep time: 10 minutes | Cook time: 5 to 6 hours | Serves 6

- 1 (10¾-ounce / 305-g) can cream of chicken soup
- 1 package dry onion soup mix
- 2½ cups water
- 1 cup long-grain rice, uncooked
- 6 ounces (170 g) boneless, skinless chicken breast tenders
- ¼ teaspoon black pepper

1. Combine all ingredients in crock pot. 2. Cook on low 5 to 6 hours. 3. Stir occasionally.

Coconut-Chicken Curry

Prep time: 15 minutes | Cook time: 7 to 8 hours | Serves 6

- 3 tablespoons extra-virgin olive oil, divided
- 1½ pounds (680 g) boneless chicken breasts
- ½ sweet onion, chopped
- 1 cup quartered baby bok choy
- 1 red bell pepper, diced
- 2 cups coconut milk
- 2 tablespoons almond butter
- 1 tablespoon red Thai curry paste
- 1 tablespoon coconut aminos
- 2 teaspoons grated fresh ginger
- Pinch red pepper flakes
- ¼ cup chopped peanuts, for garnish
- 2 tablespoons chopped cilantro, for garnish

1. Lightly grease the insert of the crock pot with 1 tablespoon of the olive oil. 2. In a large skillet over medium-high heat, heat the remaining 2 tablespoons of the olive oil. Add the chicken and brown for about 7 minutes. 3. Transfer the chicken to the crock pot and add the onion, baby bok choy, and bell pepper. 4. In a medium bowl, whisk together the coconut milk, almond butter, curry paste, coconut aminos, ginger, and red pepper flakes, until well blended. 5. Pour the sauce over the chicken and vegetables, and mix to coat. 6. Cover and cook on low for 7 to 8 hours. 7. Serve topped with the peanuts and cilantro.

Chicken with White Wine and Herbs

Prep time: 20 minutes | Cook time: 7 hours | Serves 2

- 7 bone-in, skin-on chicken thighs
- 2 tablespoons Dijon mustard
- 1 teaspoon ground paprika
- 1 teaspoon dried thyme leaves
- ½ teaspoon dried basil leaves
- 3 tablespoons all-purpose flour
- ½ teaspoon salt
- ⅛ teaspoon freshly ground black pepper
- 1 tablespoon extra-virgin olive oil
- ½ cup dry white wine
- ¼ cup chicken stock

1. On a platter, loosen the skin from the chicken. 2. In a small bowl, mix the mustard, paprika, thyme, and basil, and rub the mixture onto the chicken meat, beneath the skin. Spread the chicken skin back over this mixture and secure with toothpicks. 3. Sprinkle the chicken with the flour, salt, and pepper. 4. In a medium skillet over medium heat, heat the oil. Add the chicken, skin-side down, and brown, about 4 minutes. Do not turn the chicken over. Remove the chicken from the skillet to the crock

pot. 5. Add the wine and stock to the skillet and bring to a simmer, stirring to remove the pan drippings. 6. Pour the wine mixture over the chicken in the crock pot. 7. Cover and cook on low for 7 hours, or until the chicken registers 165°F (74°C) on a meat thermometer. 8. Remove the toothpicks and serve.

Fruit-Stuffed Turkey Thighs

Prep time: 20 minutes | Cook time: 7 hours | Serves 2

- 1 skin-on, boneless turkey thigh
- ½ teaspoon salt
- ⅛ teaspoon freshly ground black pepper
- 1 slice raisin bread, cubed
- 1 garlic clove, minced
- 2 tablespoons dark raisins
- 2 tablespoons chopped dried apricots
- 1 tablespoon water
- ½ teaspoon dried thyme
- leaves
- ½ teaspoon ground sweet paprika
- 2 teaspoons brown sugar
- 2 cups creamer potatoes
- 1 cup baby carrots
- 1 cup sliced button mushrooms
- 1 onion, chopped
- ½ cup chicken stock
- 2 tablespoons white wine vinegar

1. Place the turkey thigh on a work surface, skin-side down. Sprinkle with the salt and pepper. 2. In a small bowl, toss together the bread cubes, garlic, raisins, apricots, water, and thyme. Place the mixture on the turkey thigh. 3. Roll the turkey around the stuffing and tie the bundle closed with kitchen twine. Rub the skin with the paprika and brown sugar. 4. In the crock pot, combine the potatoes, carrots, mushrooms, and onion, and top with the turkey. Pour the stock and vinegar over everything. 5. Cover and cook on low for 7 hours, or until the turkey registers 165°F (74°C) on a meat thermometer. 6. Remove the turkey from the crock pot, and remove and discard the string. Slice and serve with the vegetables.

Chicken a la Fruit

Prep time: 20 minutes | Cook time: 6 to 8 hours | Serves 5 to 6

- ½ cup crushed pineapple, drained
- 3 whole peaches, mashed
- 2 tablespoons lemon juice
- 2 tablespoons soy sauce
- ½ to ¾ teaspoon salt
- ¼ teaspoon pepper
- 1 chicken, cut up
- Nonstick cooking spray

1. Spray crock pot with nonstick cooking spray. 2. Mix pineapple, peaches, lemon juice, soy sauce, and salt and pepper in a large bowl. 3. Dip chicken pieces in sauce and then place in crock pot. Pour remaining sauce over all. 4. Cover and cook on low 6 to 8 hours, or until chicken is tender but not dry.

Tarragon Chicken

Prep time: 25 minutes | Cook time: 3 to 5½ hours | Serves 6

- 2 tablespoons extra-virgin olive oil
- 8 chicken breast halves, skin and bones removed
- Salt and freshly ground black pepper
- 1 clove garlic, minced
- 1 medium onion, finely chopped
- 1 pound (454 g) white button mushrooms, halved
- or quartered if large
- 1 teaspoon dried tarragon
- ¼ cup dry white wine or vermouth
- 1½ cups chicken broth
- ¼ cup Dijon mustard
- ½ cup heavy cream
- 2 teaspoons cornstarch
- 2 tablespoons finely chopped fresh tarragon, plus additional for garnish

1. Heat the oil in a large skillet over high heat. Sprinkle the chicken evenly with 1 teaspoon salt and ½ teaspoon pepper. Add the chicken to the skillet and brown on all sides. Transfer the chicken to the insert of a 5- to 7-quart crock pot. 2. Add the garlic, onion, mushrooms, and dried tarragon to the skillet and sauté until the onion is softened and the mushroom liquid has evaporated, 7 to 10 minutes. Deglaze the skillet with the wine, scraping up any browned bits from the bottom. 3. Transfer the contents of the skillet to the slow-cooker insert. Add the broth and mustard to the cooker and stir to combine. Cover the crock pot and cook on high for 2½ hours or on low for 4 to 5 hours. 4. Add cream, cornstarch, and two tablespoons fresh tarragon to the crock pot and stir to combine. Cover and cook for an additional 15 minutes on high or 30 minutes on low, until the sauce is thickened. Season with salt and pepper. 5. Serve the chicken garnished with the additional fresh tarragon.

Chicken and Potatoes Barbecue

Prep time: 10 minutes | Cook time: 4 to 9 hours | Serves 8

- 8 boneless, skinless chicken breast halves, divided
- 8 small or medium potatoes, quartered, divided
- 1 cup honey barbecue sauce
- 1 (16-ounce / 454-g) can jellied cranberry sauce
- Nonfat cooking spray

1. Spray crock pot with nonstick cooking spray. Place 4 chicken breasts in crock pot. 2. Top with 4 cut-up potatoes. 3. Mix barbecue sauce and cranberry sauce together in a bowl. Spoon half the sauce over the chicken and potatoes in the cooker. 4. Place remaining breasts in cooker, followed by the remaining potato chunks. Pour rest of sauce over all. 5. Cover and cook on low 8 to 9 hours, or on high 4 hours, or until chicken and potatoes are tender but not dry.

Buffalo Chicken Stroganoff

Prep time: 10 minutes | Cook time: 7½ hours | Serves 2

- 1 onion, chopped
- 3 garlic cloves, minced
- 1 cup sliced cremini mushrooms
- 3 celery stalks, sliced
- 1 red bell pepper, sliced
- 2 tablespoons minced celery leaves
- 5 boneless, skinless chicken thighs, cubed
- 3 tablespoons all-purpose flour
- ½ teaspoon dried marjoram
- leaves
- ½ teaspoon salt
- ⅛ teaspoon freshly ground black pepper
- 1¼ cups chicken stock
- ¼ cup Buffalo wing hot sauce
- 1 bay leaf
- 3 ounces (85 g) cream cheese, cubed
- ¼ cup sour cream
- ¼ cup crumbled blue cheese

1. In the crock pot, combine the onion, garlic, mushrooms, celery, bell pepper, and celery leaves. 2. In a large bowl, toss the chicken thighs with the flour, marjoram, salt, and pepper, and place them on top of the vegetables in the crock pot. 3. In a small bowl, mix the stock with the hot sauce and bay leaf; pour the mixture into the crock pot. 4. Cover and cook on low for 7 hours, and then remove and discard the bay leaf. 5. Stir in the cream cheese and sour cream, cover, and cook on low for 20 to 30 minutes more, or until the cream cheese is melted. Gently stir. 6. Stir in the blue cheese and serve.

Chicken with Mushrooms and Shallots

Prep time: 15 minutes | Cook time: 6 to 8 hours | Serves 2

- 1 teaspoon unsalted butter, at room temperature, or extra-virgin olive oil
- 2 cups thinly sliced cremini mushrooms
- 1 teaspoon fresh thyme
- 2 garlic cloves, minced
- 1 shallot, minced
- 3 tablespoons dry sherry
- 2 bone-in, skinless chicken thighs, about 6 ounces (170 g) each
- ⅛ teaspoon sea salt
- Freshly ground black pepper

1. Grease the inside of the crock pot with the butter. 2. Put the mushrooms, thyme, garlic, and shallot into the crock pot, tossing them gently to combine. Pour in the sherry. 3. Season the chicken with the salt and pepper and place the thighs on top of the mushroom mixture. 4. Cover and cook on low for 6 to 8 hours.

Thyme Turkey Legs

Prep time: 15 minutes | Cook time: 7 to 8 hours | Serves 6

- 3 tablespoons extra-virgin olive oil, divided
- 2 pounds (907 g) boneless turkey legs
- Salt, for seasoning
- Freshly ground black pepper, for seasoning
- 1 tablespoon dried thyme
- 2 teaspoons poultry seasoning
- ½ cup chicken broth
- 2 tablespoons chopped fresh parsley, for garnish

1. Lightly grease the insert of the crock pot with 1 tablespoon of the olive oil. 2. In a large skillet over medium-high heat, heat the remaining 2 tablespoons of the olive oil. 3. Generously season the turkey with salt and pepper. Sprinkle with thyme and poultry seasoning. Add the turkey to the skillet and brown for about 7 minutes, turning once. 4. Transfer the turkey to the crock pot and add the broth. 5. Cover and cook on low for 7 to 8 hours. 6. Serve topped with the parsley.

Sweet Aromatic Chicken

Prep time: 5 minutes | Cook time: 5 to 6 hours | Serves 6 to 8

- ½ cup coconut milk
- ½ cup water
- 8 chicken thighs, skinned
- ½ cup brown sugar
- 2 tablespoons soy sauce
- ⅛ teaspoon ground cloves
- 2 garlic cloves, minced

1. Combine coconut milk and water. Pour into greased crock pot. 2. Add remaining ingredients in order listed. 3. Cover. Cook on low 5 to 6 hours.

Chicken and Shrimp Jambalaya

Prep time: 15 minutes | Cook time: 2¼ to 3¾ hours | Serves 5 to 6

- 1 (3½- to 4-pound / 1.6- to 1.8-kg) roasting chicken, cut up
- 3 onions, diced
- 1 carrot, sliced
- 3 to 4 garlic cloves, minced
- 1 teaspoon dried oregano
- 1 teaspoon dried basil
- 1 teaspoon salt
- ⅛ teaspoon white pepper
- 1 (14-ounce / 397-g) crushed tomatoes
- 1 pound (454 g) shelled raw shrimp
- 2 cups rice, cooked

1. Combine all ingredients except shrimp and rice in crock pot. 2. Cover. Cook on low 2 to 3½ hours, or until chicken is tender. 3. Add shrimp and rice. 4. Cover. Cook on high 15 to 20 minutes, or until shrimp are done.

Duck Carnitas Tacos

Prep time: 15 minutes | Cook time: 6 hours | Serves 6 to 8

- ½ cup fresh tangerine juice (or orange juice)
- 2 tablespoons fresh lime juice, plus lime wedges for serving
- 2 chipotle chiles in adobo sauce, finely chopped
- 2 garlic cloves, minced
- 1½ teaspoons coarse salt
- 6 duck legs
- Warm tortillas, chopped avocado, chopped radishes, toasted pepitas, and cilantro, for serving

1. Preheat a 5- to 6-quart crock pot. 2. Place tangerine juice, lime juice, chipotles, garlic, and salt in the crock pot, and stir until combined. Add duck, skin side up; cover, and cook on low until tender, 6 hours (or on high for 3 hours). 3. Transfer duck to a platter and let cool slightly. Remove skin; pull meat from bones in large pieces. Pour juices into a heatproof bowl; skim off fat into a separate bowl. 4. In a large nonstick skillet, heat ¼ cup reserved duck fat on high. Add duck and cook, stirring, until crisp, 6 to 7 minutes. Stir a few tablespoons of reserved juices into skillet. Serve immediately with tortillas, avocado, radishes, pepitas, and cilantro.

Old-Fashioned Chicken Pot Pie

Prep time: 15 minutes | Cook time: 4 to 5 hours | Serves 6 to 8

- 3 cups chicken broth
- 1 teaspoon dried thyme
- 4 medium Yukon gold potatoes, cut into ½-inch cubes
- 2 cups baby carrots
- 4 cups cooked chicken, cut into bite-size pieces or shredded
- 1½ cups frozen petite peas, defrosted
- 1 cup frozen white corn, defrosted
- 2 tablespoons unsalted butter, at room temperature
- 2 tablespoons all-purpose flour

1. Pour the broth in the insert of a 5- to 7-quart crock pot. Add the thyme, potatoes, and carrots, and stir to combine. Cover and cook on high for 3 to 4 hours, until the potatoes are tender. 2. Add the chicken, peas and corn and stir to combine. In a small bowl, stir the butter and flour and make a paste. Add the paste to the crock pot and stir to combine. Cover and cook for an additional 45 minutes to 1 hour, until the sauce is thickened. 3. Serve from the cooker set on warm.

Easy Chicken

Prep time: 10 minutes | Cook time: 8 hours | Serves 6 to 8

- 8 to 10 chicken wings or legs and thighs
- ½ cup soy sauce
- ½ cup sugar
- ½ teaspoon Tabasco sauce
- Pinch of ground ginger

1. Place chicken in greased crock pot. 2. Combine remaining ingredients and pour over chicken. 3. Cover. Cook on low 8 hours. 4. Serve.

Gran's Big Potluck

Prep time: 20 minutes | Cook time: 10 to 12 hours | Serves 10 to 15

- 2½ to 3 pounds (1.1 to 1.4 kg) stewing hen, cut into pieces
- ½ pound (227 g) stewing beef, cubed
- 1 (½-pound / 227-g) veal shoulder or roast, cubed
- 1½ quarts water
- ½ pound (227 g) small red potatoes, cubed
- ½ pound (227 g) small onions, cut in half
- 1 cup sliced carrots
- 1 cup chopped celery
- 1 green pepper, chopped
- 1 (1-pound / 454-g) package frozen lima beans
- 1 cup fresh or frozen okra
- 1 cup whole-kernel corn
- 1 (8-ounce / 227-g) can whole tomatoes with juice
- 1 (15-ounce / 425-g) can tomato purée
- 1 teaspoon salt
- ¼ to ½ teaspoon pepper
- 1 teaspoon dry mustard
- ½ teaspoon chili powder
- ¼ cup chopped fresh parsley

1. Combine all ingredients except last 5 seasonings in one very large crock pot, or divide between two medium-sized ones. 2. Cover. Cook on low 10 to 12 hours. Add seasonings during last hour of cooking.

Chicken Vegetable Gala

Prep time: 15 minutes | Cook time: 6 to 8 hours | Serves 4

- 4 bone-in chicken breast halves
- 1 small head of cabbage, quartered
- 1 (1-pound / 454-g)
- package baby carrots
- 2 (14½-ounce / 411-g) cans Mexican-flavored stewed tomatoes

1. Place all ingredients in crock pot in order listed. 2. Cover and cook on low 6 to 8 hours, or until chicken and vegetables are tender.

Mix-It-and-Run Chicken

Prep time: 10 minutes | Cook time: 8 to 10 hours | Serves 4

- 2 (15-ounce / 425-g) cans cut green beans, undrained
- 2 (10¾-ounce / 305-g) cans cream of mushroom soup
- 4 to 6 boneless, skinless chicken breast halves
- ½ teaspoon salt

1. Drain beans, reserving juice in a medium-sized mixing bowl. 2. Stir soups into bean juice, blending thoroughly. Set aside. 3. Place beans in crock pot. Sprinkle with salt. 4. Place chicken in cooker. Sprinkle with salt. 5. Top with soup. 6. Cover and cook on low 8 to 10 hours, or until chicken is tender, but not dry or mushy.

Hungarian Chicken

Prep time: 10 minutes | Cook time: 7 to 8 hours | Serves 4

- 1 tablespoon extra-virgin olive oil
- 2 pounds (907 g) boneless chicken thighs
- ½ cup chicken broth
- Juice and zest of 1 lemon
- 2 teaspoons minced garlic
- 2 teaspoons paprika
- ¼ teaspoon salt
- 1 cup sour cream
- 1 tablespoon chopped parsley, for garnish

1. Lightly grease the insert of the crock pot with the olive oil. 2. Place the chicken thighs in the insert. 3. In a small bowl, stir together the broth, lemon juice and zest, garlic, paprika, and salt. Pour the broth mixture over the chicken. 4. Cover and cook on low for 7 to 8 hours. 5. Turn off the heat and stir in the sour cream. 6. Serve topped with the parsley.

Slow-Cooked Turkey Dinner

Prep time: 15 minutes | Cook time: 7½ hours | Serves 4 to 6

- 1 onion, diced
- 6 small red potatoes, quartered
- 2 cups sliced carrots
- 1½ to 2 pounds (680 to 907 g) boneless, skinless turkey thighs
- ¼ cup flour
- 2 tablespoons dry onion soup mix
- 1 (10¾-ounce / 305-g) can cream of mushroom soup
- ⅔ cup chicken broth or water

1. Place vegetables in bottom of crock pot. 2. Place turkey thighs over vegetables. 3. Combine remaining ingredients. Pour over turkey. 4. Cover. Cook on high 30 minutes. Reduce heat to low and cook 7 hours.

Zesty Chicken Breasts

Prep time: 15 minutes | Cook time: 3 to 8 hours | Serves 6

- 6 bone-in chicken breast halves
- 2 (14½-ounce / 411-g) cans diced tomatoes, undrained
- 1 small can jalapeños, sliced and drained
- (optional)
- ¼ cup reduced-fat, creamy peanut butter
- 2 tablespoons fresh cilantro, chopped (optional)
- Nonfat cooking spray

1. Remove skin from chicken, but leave bone in. 2. Mix all ingredients, except chicken, in medium-sized bowl. 3. Pour one-third of sauce in bottom of crock pot sprayed with nonfat cooking spray. Place chicken on top. 4. Pour remaining sauce over chicken. 5. Cover. Cook on high 3 to 4 hours, or on low 6 to 8 hours. 6. Remove from crock pot gently. Chicken will be very tender and will fall off the bones.

Chicken Korma

Prep time: 20 minutes | Cook time: 3 to 4 hours | Serves 6

- Marinade:
- 1 tablespoon coriander seeds, ground
- 1 teaspoon salt
- 6 whole black peppercorns
- 1-inch piece fresh ginger, roughly chopped
- 3 garlic cloves, roughly chopped
- 12 boneless chicken thighs, skinned and chopped into chunks
- 1 cup Greek yogurt
- 1 heaped teaspoon gram flour
- 1 teaspoon turmeric
- Korma:
- 1 tablespoon ghee or vegetable oil
- 3 cloves
- 3 green cardamom pods
- 1-inch piece cassia bark
- 1 to 3 dried red chiles
- 2 onions, minced
- ⅓ cup creamed coconut
- 2 heaped tablespoons ground almonds
- 1 teaspoon ground white poppy seeds
- Pinch of saffron
- 2 tablespoons milk
- 1 teaspoon garam masala
- Handful fresh coriander leaves, finely chopped
- 1 tablespoon chopped toasted almonds
- Squeeze of lemon juice

Make the Marinade: 1. Place the coriander seeds, salt, and peppercorns into a mortar and pestle and crush, or grind them in a spice grinder. Then add the roughly chopped ginger and garlic, and pound (or grind) to create an aromatic paste. 2. Place the chicken in a large bowl and add the yogurt, gram flour, turmeric, and spice paste. Stir thoroughly, cover, and leave to marinate for an hour, or longer if possible, in the refrigerator. Make the Korma: 3. Heat the crock pot to high and add the oil. Add the cloves, cardamom pods, cassia bark, and the dried red chiles, and toast until fragrant, about 1 minute. 4. Add the minced onions, and then add the marinated chicken. Cover and cook for 2 hours on low, or for 1 hour on high. 5. Pour in the creamed coconut, ground almonds, and poppy seeds, then stir. Cover and cook on low for 2 more hours. 6. Crumble the saffron into a small bowl, add the milk, and leave to steep for 20 minutes. 7. Once cooked through and the sauce has thickened, pour in the saffron milk for added decadence, if using. Then add the garam masala. Garnish with the fresh coriander leaves and chopped almonds. You can also add a squeeze of lemon juice for added freshness, then serve.

Orange-Glazed Chicken Breasts

Prep time: 5 minutes | Cook time: 7¼ to 9¼ hours | Serves 6

- 1 (6-ounce / 170-g) can frozen orange juice concentrate, thawed
- ½ teaspoon dried marjoram
- 6 boneless, skinless chicken breast halves
- ¼ cup cold water
- 2 tablespoons cornstarch

1. Combine orange juice and marjoram in shallow dish. Dip each breast in orange-juice mixture and place in crock pot. Pour remaining sauce over breasts. 2. Cover. Cook on low 7 to 9 hours, or on high 3½ to 4 hours. 3. Remove chicken from crock pot. Turn cooker to high and cover. 4. Combine water and cornstarch. Stir into liquid in crock pot. Place cover slightly ajar on crock pot. Cook until sauce is thick and bubbly, about 15 to 20 minutes. Serve over chicken.

Chicken Pot Pie

Prep time: 15 minutes | Cook time: 8 hours | Serves 2

- 2 boneless, skinless chicken thighs, diced
- 1 cup diced, peeled Yukon Gold potatoes
- 1 cup frozen peas, thawed
- 1 cup diced onions
- 1 cup diced carrots
- 1 teaspoon fresh thyme
- ⅛ teaspoon sea salt
- Freshly ground black pepper
- 1 tablespoon all-purpose flour
- 1 cup low-sodium chicken broth

1. Put the chicken, potatoes, peas, onions, carrots, and thyme in the crock pot. Season with the salt and a few grinds of the pepper. Sprinkle in the flour and toss to coat the chicken and vegetables. Pour in the chicken broth. 2. Cover and cook on low for 8 hours.

Chicken Thighs with Cilantro Chutney

Prep time: 5 minutes | Cook time: 2½ hours | Serves 4 to 6

- 2 tablespoons extra-virgin olive oil
- 2 onions, coarsely chopped
- 2½ pounds (1.1 kg) boneless, skinless chicken thighs, cut into 1½-inch pieces
- Coarse salt and freshly ground pepper
- 1 tablespoon minced peeled fresh ginger
- 5 garlic cloves, thinly sliced
- 1 jalapeño chile (ribs and seeds removed for less heat, if desired), thinly sliced, plus more for serving
- 4 cups packed fresh cilantro, plus more for garnish
- ½ cup roasted peanuts, plus more, chopped, for serving
- 2 teaspoons light brown sugar
- 1 tablespoon fresh lime juice, plus wedges for serving

1. Preheat a 5- to 6-quart crock pot. 2. Heat a large skillet over medium-high. Add oil and onions; cook, stirring occasionally, until browned, about 8 minutes. Transfer to the crock pot. 3. Season chicken with salt and pepper; add to crock pot along with ginger, garlic, and jalapeño. Cover and cook on high until chicken is tender, 2 hours (or on low for 4 hours). 4. In a food processor, pulse cilantro, peanuts, brown sugar, and lime juice just until finely chopped (do not process to a paste); transfer to crock pot. Cover and continue to cook on high 30 minutes (or on low for 1 hour). Season with salt and pepper. Serve with jalapeño, cilantro, peanuts, and lime wedges.

Chicken Dijonaise

Prep time: 20 minutes | Cook time: 4 to 5 hours | Serves 8

- 3 to 4 pounds (1.4 to 1.8 kg) chicken parts (breasts, thighs, legs, or any combination), skin removed
- Salt and freshly ground black pepper
- 3 tablespoons extra-virgin olive oil
- 4 cloves garlic, minced
- 8 ounces (227 g) cipollini onions
- 1 pound (454 g) button mushrooms, cut in half if large
- 1 (16-ounce / 454-g) package frozen artichoke hearts, defrosted and quartered
- ½ cup dry white wine or vermouth
- 1½ cups chicken broth
- ⅔ cup Dijon mustard
- 1 bay leaf

1. Sprinkle the chicken evenly with 1½ teaspoons salt and ½ teaspoon pepper. Heat the oil in a large skillet over high heat. Add the chicken a few pieces at a time and brown on all sides. 2. Transfer the browned chicken to the insert of a 5- to 7-quart crock pot. Add the garlic and onions to the same skillet and sauté until the onions begin to color, about 4 minutes. Add the mushrooms and sauté until the liquid in the pan begins to evaporate, 3 to 4 minutes. 3. Add the artichoke hearts to the pan and sauté for another 3 to 4 minutes, to color the artichoke hearts. 4. Deglaze the pan with the wine, stirring up any browned bits from the bottom. Transfer the contents of the pan to the slow-cooker insert. Put the broth and mustard in a small bowl and whisk to combine. 5. Add the broth mixture to the slow-cooker insert and add the bay leaf, stirring to combine. Cover and cook on low for 4 to 5 hours, until the chicken is tender. 6. Season with salt and pepper before serving.

Barbecue Chicken for Buns

Prep time: 15 minutes | Cook time: 8 hours | Serves 16 to 20

- 6 cups diced cooked chicken
- 2 cups chopped celery
- 1 cup chopped onions
- 1 cup chopped green peppers
- 4 tablespoons butter
- 2 cups ketchup
- 2 cups water
- 2 tablespoons brown sugar
- 4 tablespoons vinegar
- 2 teaspoons dry mustard
- 1 teaspoon pepper
- 1 teaspoon salt

1. Combine all ingredients in crock pot. 2. Cover. Cook on low 8 hours. 3. Stir chicken until it shreds. 4. Serve.

Savory Stuffed Green Peppers

Prep time: 20 minutes | Cook time: 3 to 9 hours | Serves 8

- 8 small green peppers, tops removed and seeded
- 1 (10-ounce / 283-g) package frozen corn
- ¾ pound (340 g) 99% fat-free ground turkey
- ¾ pound (340 g) extra-lean ground beef
- 1 (8-ounce / 227-g) can low-sodium tomato sauce
- ½ teaspoon garlic powder
- ¼ teaspoon black pepper
- 1 cup shredded low-fat American cheese
- ½ teaspoon Worcestershire sauce
- ¼ cup chopped onions
- 3 tablespoons water
- 2 tablespoons ketchup

1. Wash peppers and drain well. Combine all ingredients except water and ketchup in mixing bowl. Stir well. 2. Stuff peppers ⅔ full. 3. Pour water in crock pot. Arrange peppers on top. 4. Pour ketchup over peppers. 5. Cover. Cook on high 3 to 4 hours, or on low 7 to 9 hours.

Cranberry Chicken

Prep time: 10 minutes | Cook time: 6 to 8 hours | Serves 6

- 6 chicken breast halves, divided
- 1 (8-ounce / 227-g) bottle Catalina or Creamy French salad dressing
- 1 envelope dry onion soup mix
- 1 (16-ounce / 454-g) can whole cranberry sauce

1. Place 3 chicken breasts in crock pot. 2. Mix other ingredients together in a mixing bowl. Pour half the sauce over chicken in the cooker. 3. Repeat Steps 1 and 2. 4. Cover and cook on low 6 to 8 hours, or until chicken is tender but not dry.

Chicken with Tropical Barbecue Sauce

Prep time: 5 minutes | Cook time: 3 to 9 hours | Serves 6

- ¼ cup molasses
- 2 tablespoons cider vinegar
- 2 tablespoons Worcestershire sauce
- 2 teaspoons prepared mustard
- ⅛ to ¼ teaspoon hot pepper sauce
- 2 tablespoons orange juice
- 3 whole chicken breasts, halved

1. Combine molasses, vinegar, Worcestershire sauce, mustard, hot pepper sauce, and orange juice. Brush over chicken. 2. Place chicken in crock pot. 3. Cover. Cook on low 7 to 9 hours, or on high 3 to 4 hours.

Italian Chicken Stew

Prep time: 20 minutes | Cook time: 3 to 6 hours | Serves 4

- 2 boneless, skinless chicken breast halves, uncooked, cut in 1½-inch pieces
- 1 (19-ounce / 539-g) can cannellini beans, drained and rinsed
- 1 (15½-ounce / 439-g) can kidney beans, drained and rinsed
- 1 (14½-ounce / 411-g) can low-sodium diced tomatoes, undrained
- 1 cup chopped celery
- 1 cup sliced carrots
- 2 small garlic cloves, coarsely chopped
- 1 cup water
- ½ cup dry red wine or low-fat chicken broth
- 3 tablespoons tomato paste
- 1 tablespoon sugar
- 1½ teaspoons dried Italian seasoning

1. Combine chicken, cannellini beans, kidney beans, tomatoes, celery, carrots, and garlic in crock pot. Mix well. 2. In medium bowl, combine all remaining ingredients. Mix well. Pour over chicken and vegetables. Mix well. 3. Cover. Cook on low 5 to 6 hours, or on high 3 hours.

Saucy Turkey Breast

Prep time: 5 minutes | Cook time: 1 to 5 hours | Serves 6 to 8

- 1 (3- to 5-pound / 1.4- to 2.3-kg) bone-in or boneless turkey breast
- 1 envelope dry onion soup mix
- Salt and pepper to taste
- 1 (16-ounce / 454-g) can cranberry sauce, jellied or whole-berry
- 2 tablespoons cornstarch
- 2 tablespoons cold water

1. Sprinkle salt and pepper and soup mix on the top and bottom of turkey breast. Place turkey in crock pot. 2. Add cranberry sauce to top of turkey breast. 3. Cover and cook on low 4 to 5 hours, or on high 1 to 3 hours, or until tender but not dry and mushy. (A meat thermometer should read 180ºF / 82ºC.) 4. Remove turkey from cooker and allow to rest for 10 minutes. (Keep sauce in cooker.) 5. Meanwhile, cover cooker and turn to high. In a small bowl, mix together cornstarch and cold water until smooth. When sauce is boiling, stir in cornstarch paste. Continue to simmer until sauce thickens. 6. Slice turkey and serve topped with sauce from cooker.

Chapter 4

Beef, Pork, and Lamb

Cajun Pork and Rice

Prep time: 29 minutes | Cook time: 5 hours | Serves 4

- 1½ teaspoons ground cumin
- 1½ teaspoons chili powder
- 1½ pounds (680 g) boneless pork loin chops
- 1 (14½-ounce / 411-g) can petite diced tomatoes, undrained
- 1 small onion, finely chopped
- 1 celery rib, finely chopped
- 1 small carrot, shredded
- 1 garlic clove, minced
- ½ teaspoon Louisiana-style hot sauce
- ¼ teaspoon salt
- 1½ cups uncooked instant rice
- 1 cup reduced-sodium chicken broth
- 1 teaspoon olive oil
- 1 medium green pepper, julienned

1. Mix cumin and chili powder; sprinkle pork chops with 2 teaspoon spice mixture. Transfer to a 4-quart crock pot. 2. In a small bowl, mix tomatoes, onion, celery, carrot, garlic, hot sauce, salt and remaining spice mixture; pour over chops. Cook, covered, on low 4 to 5 hours or until meat is tender. 3. Stir in rice and chicken broth, breaking up pork into pieces. Cook, covered, on low 10 to 15 minutes longer or until rice is tender. In a small skillet, heat oil over medium-high heat. Add green pepper; cook and stir 5 to 7 minutes or until crisp-tender. Serve with pork mixture.

Tuscan Pot Roast

Prep time: 20 minutes | Cook time: 9 hours | Serves 2

- 2 tablespoons extra-virgin olive oil
- 1½ pounds (680 g) bottom round pot roast
- 1 onion, chopped
- 2 garlic cloves, minced
- 2 carrots, sliced
- 1 cup sliced portobello mushrooms
- 2 large tomatoes, seeded
- and chopped
- 2 tablespoons chopped fresh celery leaves
- 2 tablespoons tomato paste
- ½ cup dry red wine
- ½ cup beef stock
- ½ teaspoon salt
- ½ teaspoon dried oregano
- 2 teaspoons minced fresh rosemary leaves

1. In a large skillet over medium heat, heat the oil. Add the roast and brown on both sides, turning once, about 6 minutes total. Remove from the heat. 2. In the crock pot, combine the onion, garlic, carrots, mushrooms, tomatoes, and celery leaves. Place the roast on top. 3. In a small bowl, stir together the tomato paste, wine, stock, salt, and oregano, mixing well. Pour the mixture over the roast. 4. Cover and cook on low for 8

to 9 hours, or until the beef is very tender. 5. Stir in the fresh rosemary and serve.

Pork Chops in Orange Sauce

Prep time: 25 minutes | Cook time: 5¼ to 6¼ hours | Serves 4

- 4 thick, center-cut pork chops
- Salt to taste
- Pepper to taste
- 1 tablespoon oil
- 1 orange
- ¼ cup ketchup
- ¾ cup orange juice
- 1 tablespoon orange marmalade
- 1 tablespoon cornstarch
- ¼ cup water

1. Season pork chops on both sides with salt and pepper. 2. Brown chops lightly on both sides in skillet in oil. Transfer to crock pot. Reserve 2 tablespoons drippings and discard the rest. 3. Grate ½ teaspoon orange zest from top or bottom of orange. Combine zest with ketchup, orange juice, and marmalade. Pour into skillet. Simmer 1 minute, stirring constantly. Pour over chops. 4. Cover. Cook on low 5 to 6 hours. Remove chops and keep warm. 5. Dissolve cornstarch in water. Stir into crock pot until smooth. Cook on high 15 minutes, or until thickened. 6. Serve with orange sauce on top, along with slices of fresh orange.

Cabbage and Corned Beef

Prep time: 15 minutes | Cook time: 5 to 10 hours | Serves 12

- 3 large carrots, cut into chunks
- 1 cup chopped celery
- 1 teaspoon salt
- ½ teaspoon black pepper
- 1 cup water
- 1 (4-pound / 1.8-kg) corned
- beef
- 1 large onion, cut into pieces
- 4 potatoes, peeled and chunked
- Half a small head of cabbage, cut in wedges

1. Place carrots, celery, seasonings, and water in crock pot. 2. Add beef. Cover with onions. 3. Cover. Cook on low 8 to 10 hours, or on high 5 to 6 hours. (If your schedule allows, this dish has especially good taste and texture if you begin it on high for 1 hour, and then turn it to low for 5 to 6 hours, before going on to Step 4.) 4. Lift corned beef out of cooker and add potatoes, pushing them to bottom of crock pot. Return beef to cooker. 5. Cover. Cook on low 1 hour. 6. Lift corned beef out of cooker and add cabbage, pushing the wedges down into the broth. Return beef to cooker. 7. Cover. Cook on low 1 more hour. 8. Remove corned beef. Cool and slice on the diagonal. Serve surrounded by vegetables.

Shredded Beef for Tacos

Prep time: 15 minutes | Cook time: 6 to 8 hours | Serves 6 to 8

- 1 (2- to 3-pound / 907-g to 1.4-kg) round roast, cut into large chunks
- 1 large onion, chopped
- 3 tablespoons oil
- 2 serrano chilies, chopped
- 3 garlic cloves, minced
- 1 teaspoon salt
- 1 cup water

1. Brown meat and onion in oil. Transfer to crock pot. 2. Add chilies, garlic, salt, and water. 3. Cover. Cook on high 6 to 8 hours. 4. Pull meat apart with two forks until shredded. 5. Serve.

Cedric's Casserole

Prep time: 30 minutes | Cook time: 3 to 4 hours | Serves 4 to 6

- 1 medium onion, chopped
- 3 tablespoons butter or margarine
- 1 pound (454 g) ground beef
- ½ to ¾ teaspoon salt
- ¼ teaspoon pepper
- 3 cups shredded cabbage
- 1 (10¾-ounce / 305-g) can tomato soup

1. Sauté onion in skillet in butter. 2. Add ground beef and brown. Season with salt and pepper. 3. Layer half of cabbage in crock pot, followed by half of meat mixture. Repeat layers. 4. Pour soup over top. 5. Cover. Cook on low 3 to 4 hours. 6. Serve.

Slow-Cooked Coffee Beef Roast

Prep time: 20 minutes | Cook time: 8 to 10 hours | Serves 12

- 1½ pounds (680 g) boneless beef sirloin tip roast, cut in half
- 2 teaspoons canola oil
- 1½ cups sliced fresh mushrooms
- ½ cup sliced green onions
- 2 garlic cloves, minced
- 1½ cups brewed coffee
- 1 teaspoon liquid smoke (optional)
- ½ teaspoon salt
- ½ teaspoon chili powder
- ¼ teaspoon black pepper
- ¼ cup cornstarch
- ½ cup cold water

1. In a large nonstick skillet, brown roast over medium-high heat on all sides in oil. Transfer roast to crock pot. 2. In the same skillet, sauté mushrooms, onions, and garlic until tender. 3. Stir the coffee, liquid smoke if desired, salt, chili powder, and pepper into the vegetables. Pour over roast. 4. Cook on low for 8 to 10 hours or until meat is tender. 5. Remove roast and keep warm. 6. Pour cooking juices into a 2-cup measuring cup; skim fat. 7. Combine cornstarch and water in a saucepan until smooth. Gradually stir in 2 cups of cooking juices. 8. Bring to a boil; cook and stir for 2 minutes or until thickened. Serve with sliced beef.

Lamb Shanks and Potatoes

Prep time: 10 minutes | Cook time: 5 to 8 hours | Serves 6

- 1 (15-ounce / 425-g) can crushed tomatoes in purée
- 3 tablespoons tomato paste
- 2 tablespoons apricot jam
- 6 cloves garlic, thinly sliced
- 3 strips orange zest
- ¾ teaspoon crushed dried rosemary
- ½ teaspoon ground ginger
- ½ teaspoon ground
- cinnamon
- Coarse sea salt
- Black pepper
- 3½ pounds (1.6 kg) lamb shanks, trimmed of excess fat and cut into 1½-inch slices
- 1¼ pounds (567 g) small new potatoes, halved (or quartered, if large)

1. Stir together the tomatoes and purée, tomato paste, jam, garlic, orange zest, rosemary, ginger, and cinnamon in the crock pot. Season with salt and pepper. 2. Add the lamb and potatoes, and spoon the tomato mixture over the lamb to coat. 3. Cover and cook until the lamb and potatoes are tender, on low for 8 hours or on high for 5 hours. Season again with salt and pepper, if desired. 4. Serve hot.

Mexican Casserole

Prep time: 15 minutes | Cook time: 8 to 9 hours | Serves 8

- 1 pound (454 g) extra-lean ground beef
- 1 medium onion, chopped
- 1 small green bell pepper, chopped
- 1 (16-ounce / 454-g) can kidney beans, rinsed and drained
- 1 (14½-ounce / 411-g) can diced tomatoes, undrained
- 1 (8-ounce / 227-g) can tomato sauce
- ¼ cup water
- 1 envelope reduced-sodium taco seasoning
- 1 tablespoon chili powder
- 1⅓ cups instant rice, uncooked
- 1 cup low-fat Cheddar cheese

1. Brown ground beef and onion in nonstick skillet. 2. Combine all ingredients in crock pot except rice and cheese. 3. Cook on low 8 to 9 hours. 4. Stir in rice, cover, and cook until tender. 5. Sprinkle with cheese. Cover and cook until cheese is melted. Serve.

Easy Beef Tortillas

Prep time: 20 minutes | Cook time: 1½ to 3 hours | Serves 6

- 1½ pounds (680 g) ground beef
- 1 (10¾-ounce / 305-g) can cream of chicken soup
- 2½ cups crushed tortilla chips, divided
- 1 (16-ounce / 454-g) jar salsa
- 1½ cups shredded Cheddar cheese
- Nonstick cooking spray

1. Brown ground beef in a nonstick skillet. Drain. Stir in soup. 2. Spray inside of cooker with nonstick cooking spray. Sprinkle 1½ cups tortilla chips in crock pot. Top with beef mixture, then salsa, and then cheese. 3. Cover and cook on high for 1½ hours, or on low for 3 hours. 4. Sprinkle with remaining chips just before serving.

Corned Beef and Cabbage Braised in Riesling

Prep time: 20 minutes | Cook time: 8 to 10 hours | Serves 6

- 12 small Yukon gold potatoes, scrubbed
- 2 cups baby carrots
- 3 medium sweet onions, such as Vidalia, coarsely chopped
- 2 cups Riesling wine
- ½ cup whole-grain mustard
- ¼ cup Dijon mustard
- ¼ cup firmly packed light
- brown sugar
- 4 whole black peppercorns
- 2 bay leaves
- 1 (3½- to 4-pound / 1.6- to 1.8-kg) corned beef, rinsed and fat trimmed
- 1 large head green cabbage, cut in half, cored and thickly sliced

1. Layer the potatoes, carrots, and onions in the insert of a 5- to 7-quart crock pot. Whisk together the riesling, mustards, and sugar in a large bowl. Stir in the peppercorns and bay leaves. 2. Place the brisket on top of the vegetables in the slow-cooker insert. (If you are using a 5-quart cooker, you may need to cut the brisket in half and stack the pieces to fit.) Pour the riesling mixture over the brisket and strew the cabbage over the top of the brisket. 3. Cover the crock pot and cook on low for 8 to 10 hours. Remove the brisket from the cooker, cover with aluminum foil, and allow to rest for about 20 minutes. 4. Using a slotted spoon, remove the vegetables and arrange them on a platter. Slice the brisket across the grain and arrange over the vegetables. Strain the liquid from the cooker through a fine-mesh sieve and ladle a bit over the meat and vegetables before serving.

Meat Loaf and Mushrooms

Prep time: 20 minutes | Cook time: 5 hours | Serves 6

- 2 (1-ounce / 28-g) slices whole wheat bread
- ½ pound (227 g) extra-lean ground beef
- ¾ pound (340 g) fat-free ground turkey
- 1½ cups mushrooms, sliced
- ½ cup minced onions
- 1 teaspoon Italian
- seasoning
- ¾ teaspoon salt
- 2 eggs
- 1 clove garlic, minced
- 3 tablespoons ketchup
- 1½ teaspoons Dijon mustard
- ⅛ teaspoon ground red pepper

1. Fold two strips of tin foil, each long enough to fit from the top of the cooker, down inside and up the other side, plus a 2-inch overhang on each side of the cooker—to function as handles for lifting the finished loaf out of the cooker. 2. Process bread slices in food processor until crumbs measure 1⅓ cups. 3. Combine bread crumbs, beef, turkey, mushrooms, onions, Italian seasoning, salt, eggs, and garlic in bowl. Shape into loaf to fit in crock pot. 4. Mix together ketchup, mustard, and pepper. Spread over top of loaf. 5. Cover. Cook on low 5 hours. 6. When finished, pull loaf up gently with foil handles. Place loaf on warm platter. Pull foil handles away. Allow loaf to rest for 10 minutes before slicing.

Mediterranean-Style Spareribs

Prep time: 15 minutes | Cook time: 8 to 10 hours | Serves 6

- 3 pounds (1.4 kg) country-style spareribs
- 1½ teaspoons salt
- 2 tablespoons extra-virgin olive oil
- 3 medium onions, finely chopped
- ⅛ teaspoon red pepper
- flakes
- 3 cloves garlic, minced
- 1 teaspoon dried oregano
- ½ cup red wine, such as Chianti or Barolo
- 1 (28- to 32-ounce / 794- to 907-g) can crushed tomatoes, with their juice

1. Sprinkle the ribs with the salt and arrange in the insert of a 5- to 7-quart crock pot. Heat the oil in a large skillet over medium-high heat. Add the onions, red pepper flakes, garlic, and oregano and sauté until the onions are softened, about 5 minutes. 2. Add the wine to the skillet and stir up any browned bits from the bottom of the pan. Transfer the contents of the skillet to the slow-cooker insert and stir in the tomatoes. Cover and cook on low for 8 to 10 hours, until the meat is tender. Skim off any fat from the surface of the sauce. 3. Serve the ribs from the cooker set on warm.

Three-Ingredient Sauerkraut Meal

Prep time: 5 minutes | Cook time: 8 to 10 hours | Serves 8

- 2 cups low-sodium barbecue sauce
- 1 cup water
- 2 pounds (907 g) thinly sliced lean pork chops, trimmed of fat
- 2 pounds (907 g) sauerkraut, rinsed

1. Mix together barbecue sauce and water. 2. Combine barbecue sauce, pork chops, and sauerkraut in crock pot. 3. Cover. Cook on low 8 to 10 hours

Asian Pork Spare Ribs

Prep time: 10 minutes | Cook time: 9 to 10 hours | Serves 4

- 1 tablespoon extra-virgin olive oil
- 2 pounds (907 g) pork spare ribs
- 1 tablespoon Chinese five-spice powder
- 2 teaspoons garlic powder
- ½ cup chicken broth
- 3 tablespoons coconut aminos
- 3 tablespoons sesame oil
- 2 tablespoons apple cider vinegar
- 1 tablespoon granulated erythritol

1. Lightly grease the insert of the crock pot with the olive oil. 2. Season the ribs with the five-spice powder and garlic powder, and place upright on their ends in the insert. 3. Add the broth, coconut aminos, sesame oil, apple cider vinegar, and erythritol to the bottom of the insert, stirring to blend. 4. Cover and cook on low for 9 to 10 hours. 5. Serve warm.

Meal-in-One

Prep time: 25 minutes | Cook time: 4 hours | Serves 6 to 8

- 2 pounds (907 g) ground beef
- 1 onion, diced
- 1 green bell pepper, diced
- 1 teaspoon salt
- ¼ teaspoon pepper
- 1 large bag frozen hash brown potatoes
- 1 (16-ounce / 454-g) container sour cream
- 1 (24-ounce / 680-g) container cottage cheese
- 1 cup Monterey Jack cheese, shredded

1. Brown ground beef, onion, and green pepper in skillet. Drain. Season with salt and pepper. 2. In crock pot, layer one-third of the potatoes, meat, sour cream, and cottage cheese. Repeat twice. 3. Cover. Cook on low 4 hours, sprinkling Monterey Jack cheese over top during last hour. 4. Serve.

German Pot Roast

Prep time: 15 minutes | Cook time: 4 to 8 hours | Serves 12

- 2 pounds (907 g) boneless, lean pork roast
- 1 teaspoon garlic salt
- ½ teaspoon black pepper
- 4 large sweet potatoes, peeled and diced
- 2 medium onions, sliced
- ½ teaspoon dried oregano
- 1 (14½-ounce / 411-g) can low-sodium tomatoes

1. Place pork roast in crock pot. 2. Sprinkle with garlic salt and pepper. 3. Add remaining ingredients. 4. Cover. Cook on low 7 to 8 hours, or on high 4 to 5 hours.

Chili Casserole

Prep time: 25 minutes | Cook time: 7 hours | Serves 6

- 1 pound (454 g) bulk pork sausage, browned
- 2 cups water
- 1 (15½-ounce / 439-g) can chili beans
- 1 (14½-ounce / 411-g) can diced tomatoes
- ¾ cup brown rice
- ¼ cup chopped onions
- 1 tablespoon chili powder
- 1 teaspoon Worcestershire sauce
- 1 teaspoon prepared mustard
- ¾ teaspoon salt
- ⅛ teaspoon garlic powder
- 1 cup shredded Cheddar cheese

1. Combine all ingredients except cheese in crock pot. 2. Cover. Cook on low 7 hours. 3. Stir in cheese during last 10 minutes of cooking time.

Smothered Steak

Prep time: 10 minutes | Cook time: 8 hours | Serves 6

- 1 (1½-pound / 680-g) chuck or round steak, cut into strips
- ⅓ cup flour
- ½ teaspoon salt
- ¼ teaspoon pepper
- 1 large onion, sliced
- 1 to 2 green peppers, sliced
- 1 (14½-ounce / 411-g) can stewed tomatoes
- 1 (4-ounce / 113-g) can mushrooms, drained
- 2 tablespoons soy sauce
- 1 (10-ounce / 283-g) package frozen French-style green beans

1. Layer steak in bottom of crock pot. Sprinkle with flour, salt, and pepper. Stir well to coat steak. 2. Add remaining ingredients. Mix together gently. 3. Cover. Cook on low 8 hours. 4. Serve.

Spanish-Style Lamb Chops

Prep time: 15 minutes | Cook time: 8 hours | Serves 2

- 1 teaspoon extra-virgin olive oil
- ½ cup diced onion
- ½ cup diced roasted red pepper
- 2 tablespoons fresh parsley
- ½ cup red wine
- ⅛ teaspoon sea salt
- Freshly ground black
- pepper
- 1 teaspoon minced garlic
- ½ teaspoon minced fresh rosemary
- 1 teaspoon smoked paprika
- 2 bone-in lamb shoulders, trimmed of fat
- 2 red potatoes, unpeeled, quartered

1. Grease the inside of the crock pot with the olive oil. 2. Put the onion, red pepper, parsley, and wine into the crock pot. 3. In a small bowl, combine the salt, a few grinds of the black pepper, garlic, rosemary, and paprika. Rub this mixture over the lamb chops. For even better flavor, do this one day ahead to allow all the flavors of the rub to permeate the meat. Place the chops into the crock pot on top of the onion and wine mixture. The chops may need to slightly overlap one another to fit. 4. Place the potatoes on top of the lamb. 5. Cover and cook on low for 8 hours.

Taters 'n Beef

Prep time: 20 minutes | Cook time: 4¼ to 6¼ hours | Serves 6 to 8

- 2 pounds (907 g) ground beef, browned
- 1 teaspoon salt
- ½ teaspoon pepper
- ¼ cup chopped onions
- 1 cup canned tomato soup
- 6 potatoes, sliced
- 1 cup milk

1. Combined beef, salt, pepper, onions, and soup. 2. Place a layer of potatoes in bottom of crock pot. Cover with a portion of the meat mixture. Repeat layers until ingredients are used. 3. Cover. Cook on low 4 to 6 hours. Add milk and cook on high 15 to 20 minutes.

Ham and Chunky Potatoes

Prep time: 5 minutes | Cook time: 10 hours | Serves 6 to 8

- 6 to 8 medium red or russet potatoes, cut into chunks
- 1 (2- to 3-pound / 907-g to
- 1.4-kg) boneless ham
- ½ cup brown sugar
- 1 teaspoon dry mustard

1. Prick potato pieces with fork. Place in crock pot. 2. Place ham on top of potatoes. Crumble brown sugar over ham.

Sprinkle with dry mustard. 3. Cover. Cook on low 10 or more hours, until potatoes are tender. 4. Pour juices over ham and potatoes to serve.

Sausage Lasagna

Prep time: 15 minutes | Cook time: 4 to 6 hours | Serves 8

- 1 pound (454 g) Italian pork sausage, casings removed
- 1 pound (454 g) ground beef sirloin
- 1 medium yellow onion, finely chopped
- 2 medium carrots, finely chopped
- 2 cloves garlic, minced
- Coarse sea salt
- Black pepper
- 1 (6-ounce / 170-g) can tomato paste
- 1 (28-ounce / 794-g) can crushed tomatoes in purée
- 9 ounces (255 g) lasagna noodles
- 2 cups shredded part-skim Mozzarella cheese (about 8 ounces / 227 g)

1. In a 5-quart Dutch oven or large heavy pot, cook the sausage and beef over medium-high, breaking up the meat with a wooden spoon. Cook, stirring often, until no longer pink, 4 to 6 minutes. 2. Add the onion, carrots, and garlic, and season with the salt and pepper. Cook until the onion has softened, 3 to 5 minutes. 3. Stir in the tomato paste, then the tomatoes. Bring to a boil, and remove from the heat. 4. Spoon 2 cups of the meat mixture into the bottom of the crock pot. Layer 3 noodles (breaking them, as needed, to fit), 2 cups meat mixture, and ½ cup Mozzarella. Repeat, with two more layers. Refrigerate the remaining ½ cup Mozzarella for topping. 5. Cover and cook on low for 4 to 6 hours. Sprinkle the lasagna with the remaining ½ cup Mozzarella. Cover and cook until the cheese has melted, about 10 minutes. 6. Serve hot.

Pigs in Blankets

Prep time: 30 minutes | Cook time: 6 to 8 hours | Serves 4

- 1 (1- to 2-pound / 454 to 907-g) round steak
- 1 pound (454 g) bacon
- 1 cup ketchup
- ¼ cup brown sugar
- 1 small onion
- ¼ to ½ cup water

1. Cut round steak into long strips. Roll up each meat strip, and then wrap with a slice of bacon. Secure with a toothpick to hold the roll shape. 2. Warm remaining ingredients in saucepan, bringing to a simmer to make a sauce. 3. Place meat rolls in crock pot. Pour sauce over top. 4. Cover and cook on low 6 to 8 hours, or until the meat is tender but not overcooked.

Pork Chops with Tomato Sauce

Prep time: 25 minutes | Cook time: 3 to 7 hours | Serves 4 to 6

- 4 thickly-cut pork chops
- 1 medium onion, sliced or chopped
- ½ cup ketchup
- ¼ cup brown sugar
- ½ teaspoon chili powder
- ½ cup water

1. Place pork chops in bottom of crock pot. Top with onions. 2. In a bowl, mix ketchup, brown sugar, chili powder and water together. Spoon sauce over all. (If the chops need to be stacked in order to fit into your cooker, make sure to top each one with sauce.) 3. Cover and cook on high 3 to 4 hours, or on low for up to 6 to 7 hours, or until meat is tender but not dry.

Low-Fat crock pot Barbecue

Prep time: 20 minutes | Cook time: 4 hours | Serves 12

- 1 pound (454 g) extra-lean ground beef
- 2 cups celery, chopped fine
- 1 cup onions, chopped
- 1 tablespoon whipped butter
- 2 tablespoons red wine vinegar
- 1 tablespoon brown sugar
- 3 tablespoons Worcestershire sauce
- 1 teaspoon salt
- 1 teaspoon yellow prepared mustard
- 1 cup ketchup
- 2 cups water

1. Brown ground beef, celery, and onions in a nonstick skillet. 2. Combine all ingredients in crock pot. 3. Cover and cook on high for 4 hours. 4. Serve.

Lemon Pork

Prep time: 15 minutes | Cook time: 7 to 8 hours | Serves 6

- 3 tablespoons extra-virgin olive oil, divided
- 1 tablespoon butter
- 2 pounds (907 g) pork loin roast
- ½ teaspoon salt
- ¼ teaspoon freshly ground
- black pepper
- ¼ cup chicken broth
- Juice and zest of 1 lemon
- 1 tablespoon minced garlic
- ½ cup heavy (whipping) cream

1. Lightly grease the insert of the crock pot with 1 tablespoon of the olive oil. 2. In a large skillet over medium-high heat, heat the remaining 2 tablespoons of the olive oil and the butter. 3. Lightly season the pork with salt and pepper. Add the

pork to the skillet and brown the roast on all sides for about 10 minutes. Transfer it to the insert. 4. In a small bowl, stir together the broth, lemon juice and zest, and garlic. 5. Add the broth mixture to the roast. 6. Cover, and cook on low for 7 to 8 hours. 7. Stir in the heavy cream and serve.

Dijon Pork Chops

Prep time: 10 minutes | Cook time: 8 hours | Serves 4

- 1 tablespoon extra-virgin olive oil
- 1 cup chicken broth
- 1 sweet onion, chopped
- ¼ cup Dijon mustard
- 1 teaspoon minced garlic
- 1 teaspoon maple extract
- 4 (4 ounces / 113 g) boneless pork chops
- 1 cup heavy (whipping) cream
- 1 teaspoon chopped fresh thyme, for garnish

1. Lightly grease the insert of the crock pot with the olive oil. 2. Add the broth, onion, Dijon mustard, garlic, and maple extract to the insert, and stir to combine. Add the pork chops. 3. Cover and cook on low for 8 hours. 4. Stir in the heavy cream. 5. Serve topped with the thyme.

Crock Pot Swiss Steak

Prep time: 30 minutes | Cook time: 7 hours | Serves 4

- 1 (1-pound / 454-g) round steak, ¾ to 1-inch thick, cubed
- 1 (16-ounce / 454-g) can stewed tomatoes
- 3 carrots, halved lengthwise
- 2 potatoes, quartered
- 1 medium onion, quartered
- Garlic powder to taste (optional)

1. Add all ingredients to your crock pot in the order they are listed. 2. Cover and cook on low for 7 hours, or until meat and vegetables are tender, but not overcooked or dry.

Creamy Hamburger Topping

Prep time: 15 minutes | Cook time: 3 to 5 hours | Serves 8

- 1 pound (454 g) ground beef
- 8 ounces (227 g) shredded cheese, your choice of flavors
- 1 onion, diced
- 1 (10¾-ounce / 305-g) can cream of mushroom soup
- 1 (12-ounce / 340-g) can diced tomatoes, undrained

1. Brown ground beef in a nonstick skillet. Drain. 2. Combine all ingredients in your crock pot. 3. Cook on low 3 to 5 hours, or until heated through. 4. Serve.

Beef and Black Bean Chili

Prep time: 15 minutes | Cook time: 6 hours | Serves 4

- 1 cup dried black beans, picked over and rinsed
- 1 pound (454 g) beef chuck, cut into ¾-inch chunks
- 1 (15-ounce / 425-g) can tomato puree
- 1 red onion, finely chopped
- 2 garlic cloves, minced
- 3 tablespoons chili powder
- 2 cups hot water
- Coarse salt and freshly ground pepper
- Sour cream, diced jalapeño, chopped avocado, and grated cheddar cheese or crumbled queso fresco, for serving

1. Place beans in a bowl; cover with water by several inches. Refrigerate, covered, overnight; drain. 2. Preheat a 5- to 6-quart crock pot. 3. Add beans. Add beef, tomato puree, onion (reserve 1 tablespoon for garnish), garlic, chili powder, the hot water, 2 teaspoons salt, and ½ teaspoon pepper and stir to combine. Cover and cook on high until chili has thickened and beans are tender, 6 hours (or on low for 8 hours). Serve with sour cream, reserved onion, jalapeño, avocado, and cheese.

Pork Chops with Sauerkraut and Apples

Prep time: 10 minutes | Cook time: 3½ to 8 hours | Serves 6

- ½ cup (1 stick) unsalted butter, melted
- 4 Braeburn apples, peeled, cored, cut into ½-inch-thick slices
- ½ cup Dijon mustard
- ½ cup firmly packed light brown sugar
- 6 (1-inch-thick) pork loin chops
- 2 medium sweet onions, cut into half moons
- 1 (1-pound / 454-g) bag sauerkraut, rinsed and drained
- ½ cup apple juice

1. Pour half the butter into the insert of a 5- to 7-quart crock pot. Add the apples and toss to coat. Stir the mustard and sugar together in a small bowl and dot the apples with ¼ cup of the mustard mixture. 2. Paint the pork chops with the remaining mustard mixture and put the pork chops on the apples. Heat the remaining butter in a large skillet over medium-high heat. Add the onions and sauté until they begin to turn golden, about 15 minutes. 3. Add the sauerkraut to the onions and stir to combine. Spread the sauerkraut mixture over the pork and pour in the apple juice. Cover and cook on high for 3½ to 4 hours or on low for 6 to 8 hours, until the pork is tender and cooked through. 4. Serve the pork chops with the apples and sauerkraut.

Burgundy Pot Roast

Prep time: 15 minutes | Cook time: 9 to 11 hours | Serves 8 to 10

- 2 beef bouillon cubes
- ¼ cup boiling water
- 1 (14½-ounce / 411-g) can low-sodium diced or stewed tomatoes
- 1 cup dry red wine or burgundy
- 1 (1.8-ounce / 51-g) box dry leek soup mix
- 1 tablespoon Worcestershire sauce
- 4 cloves garlic, crushed or
- sliced
- 1 teaspoon dried rosemary
- 1 teaspoon dried thyme
- 1 teaspoon dried marjoram
- 3 pounds (1.4 kg) lean boneless beef pot roast, rolled and tied
- 2½ cups sliced carrots
- ½ cup parsnips, peeled, halved crosswise
- 4 tablespoons flour
- ⅓ cup cold water

1. Dissolve bouillon cubes in boiling water. Pour into crock pot. 2. Stir in tomatoes, wine, dry soup mix, Worcestershire sauce, garlic, and herbs. 3. Add meat. Roll in liquid to coat. 4. Put vegetables around meat. 5. Cover. Cook on low 9 to 11 hours. 6. Remove meat to plate. Cover to keep warm. Turn crock pot to high. 7. Whisk flour into ⅓ cup cold water. Stir into liquid and cook, covered, for 10 minutes. 8. Serve meat sliced.

Mexican Goulash

Prep time: 45 minutes | Cook time: 3 to 4 hours | Serves 8 to 10

- 1½ to 2 pounds (680 to 907 g) ground beef
- 2 onions, chopped
- 1 green pepper, chopped
- ½ cup celery, chopped
- 1 garlic clove, minced
- 1 (28-ounce / 794-g) can whole tomatoes, cut up
- 1 (6-ounce / 170-g) can tomato paste
- 1 (4¼-ounce / 120-g) can sliced black olives, drained
- 1 (14½-ounce / 411-g) can
- green beans, drained
- 1 (15¼-ounce / 432-g) can Mexicorn, drained
- 1 (15-ounce / 425-g) can dark red kidney beans
- Diced jalapeño peppers to taste
- 1 teaspoon salt
- ¼ teaspoon pepper
- 1 tablespoon chili powder
- 3 dashes Tabasco sauce
- Shredded Cheddar cheese

1. Brown ground beef. Reserve drippings and transfer beef to crock pot. 2. Sauté onions, pepper, celery, and garlic in drippings in skillet. Transfer to crock pot. Add remaining ingredients except cheese. Mix well. 3. Cover. Cook on high 3 to 4 hours. 4. Sprinkle individual servings with shredded cheese. Serve.

Easy Stroganoff

Prep time: 5 minutes | Cook time: 6¼ to 8¼ hours | Serves 6 to 8

- 1 (10¾-ounce / 305-g) can cream of mushroom soup
- 1 (14½-ounce / 411-g) can beef broth
- 1 pound (454 g) beef
- stewing meat or round steak, cut in 1-inch pieces
- 1 cup sour cream
- 2 cups noodles, cooked

1. Combine soup and broth in crock pot. Add meat. 2. Cover. Cook on high 3 to 4 hours. Reduce heat to low and cook 3 to 4 hours. 3. Stir in sour cream. 4. Stir in noodles. 5. Cook on high 20 minutes.

Beef Stew Bourguignonne

Prep time: 15 minutes | Cook time: 10¼ to 12¼ hours | Serves 6

- 2 pounds (907 g) stewing beef, cut in 1-inch cubes
- 2 tablespoons cooking oil
- 1 (10¾-ounce / 305-g) can condensed golden cream of mushroom soup
- 1 teaspoon Worcestershire sauce
- ⅓ cup dry red wine
- ½ teaspoon dried oregano
- 2 teaspoons salt
- ½ teaspoon pepper
- ½ cup chopped onions
- ½ cup chopped carrots
- 1 (4-ounce / 113-g) can mushroom pieces, drained
- ½ cup cold water
- ¼ cup flour
- Noodles, cooked

1. Brown meat in oil in saucepan. Transfer to crock pot. 2. Mix together soup, Worcestershire sauce, wine, oregano, salt and pepper, onions, carrots, and mushrooms. Pour over meat. 3. Cover. Cook on low 10 to 12 hours. 4. Combine water and flour. Stir into beef mixture. Turn cooker to high. 5. Cook and stir until thickened and bubbly. 6. Serve over noodles.

African Beef Curry

Prep time: 20 minutes | Cook time: 6 to 8 hours | Serves 6

- 1 pound (454 g) extra-lean ground beef, browned
- 1 large onion, thinly sliced
- 1 green bell pepper, diced
- 1 tomato, peeled and diced
- 1 apple, peeled, cored, and diced
- 1 to 2 teaspoons curry (or more to taste)
- 4 cups prepared rice

1. Spray crock pot with fat-free cooking spray. 2. Add all ingredients except rice in crock pot and mix well. 3. Cover and cook on high 6 to 8 hours. 4. Serve over hot rice.

Conga Lime Pork

Prep time: 20 minutes | Cook time: 4 hours | Serves 6

- 1 teaspoon salt, divided
- ½ teaspoon pepper, divided
- 1 (2- to 3-pound / 907-g to 1.4-kg) boneless pork shoulder butt roast
- 1 tablespoon canola oil
- 1 large onion, chopped
- 3 garlic cloves, peeled and thinly sliced
- ½ cup water
- 2 chipotle peppers in adobo
- sauce, seeded and chopped
- 2 tablespoons molasses
- 2 cups broccoli coleslaw mix
- 1 medium mango, peeled and chopped
- 2 tablespoons lime juice
- 1½ teaspoons grated lime peel
- 6 prepared corn muffins, halved

1. Sprinkle ¾ teaspoon salt and ¼ teaspoon pepper over roast. In a large skillet, brown pork in oil on all sides. Transfer meat to a 3- or 4-quart crock pot. 2. In the same skillet, saute onion until tender. Add garlic; cook 1 minute longer. Add water, chipotle peppers and molasses, stirring to loosen browned bits from pan. Pour over pork. Cover and cook on high for 4 to 5 hours or until meat is tender. 3. Remove roast; cool slightly. Skim fat from cooking juices. Shred pork with two forks and return to crock pot; heat through. In a large bowl, combine the coleslaw mix, mango, lime juice, lime peel and remaining salt and pepper. 4. Place muffin halves cut side down on an ungreased baking sheet. Broil 4 inch from the heat for 2 to 3 minutes or until lightly toasted. Serve pork with muffins; top with slaw.

Beef and Lentils

Prep time: 35 minutes | Cook time: 6 to 8 hours | Serves 12

- 1 medium onion
- 3 whole cloves
- 5 cups water
- 1 pound (454 g) lentils
- 1 teaspoon salt
- 1 bay leaf
- 1 pound (454 g) (or less) ground beef, browned and
- drained
- ½ cup ketchup
- ¼ cup molasses
- 2 tablespoons brown sugar
- 1 teaspoon dry mustard
- ¼ teaspoon Worcestershire sauce
- 1 onion, finely chopped

1. Stick cloves into whole onion. Set aside. 2. In large saucepan, combine water, lentils, salt, bay leaf, and whole onion with cloves. Simmer 30 minutes. 3. Meanwhile, combine all remaining ingredients in crock pot. Stir in simmered ingredients from saucepan. Add additional water if mixture seems dry. 4. Cover. Cook on low 6 to 8 hours (check to see if lentils are tender).

Hawaiian Sausages

Prep time: 15 minutes | Cook time: 4 to 5 hours | Serves 6 to 8

- 3 pounds (1.4 kg) link pork sausages
- 2 cups pineapple juice
- 3 tablespoons cornstarch
- 1 teaspoon curry powder
- 1 ripe large pineapple, peeled and cored, and cut into 1-inch chunks (about 4 cups)

1. Sauté the sausages in a large skillet until browned on all sides. Transfer the sausages to the insert of a 5- to 7-quart crock pot. 2. Mix the pineapple juice, cornstarch, and curry powder in a mixing bowl, and pour into the slow-cooker insert. Add the pineapple, cover, and cook on low for 4 to 5 hours, until the sausages are cooked through and the sauce is thickened. 3. Serve from the cooker set on warm.

Chapter ⑤

Fish and Seafood

Bayou Gulf Shrimp Gumbo

Prep time: 35 minutes | Cook time: 5 hours | Serves 6

- ½ pound (227 g) bacon strips, chopped
- 3 celery ribs, chopped
- 1 medium onion, chopped
- 1 medium green pepper, chopped
- 2 garlic cloves, minced
- 2 (8-ounce / 227-g) bottles clam juice
- 1 (14½-ounce / 411-g) can diced tomatoes, undrained
- 2 tablespoons Worcestershire sauce
- 1 teaspoon kosher salt
- 1 teaspoon dried marjoram
- 2 pounds (907 g) uncooked large shrimp, peeled and deveined
- 2½ cups frozen sliced okra, thawed
- Hot cooked rice

1. In a large skillet, cook bacon over medium heat until crisp. Remove to paper towels with a slotted spoon; drain, reserving 2 tablespoons drippings. Saute the celery, onion, green pepper and garlic in drippings until tender. 2. Transfer to a 4-quart crock pot. Stir in the bacon, clam juice, tomatoes, Worcestershire sauce, salt and marjoram. Cover and cook on low for 4 hours. 3. Stir in shrimp and okra. Cover and cook 1 hour longer or until shrimp turn pink and okra is heated through. Serve with rice.

Shrimp and Artichoke Barley Risotto

Prep time: 15 minutes | Cook time: 3 hours | Serves 4

- 3 cups seafood stock (or chicken stock)
- 1 teaspoon olive oil
- 1 yellow onion, chopped
- 3 cloves garlic, minced
- 1 (9-ounce / 255-g) package frozen artichoke hearts, thawed and quartered
- 1 cup uncooked pearl
- barley
- Black pepper
- 1 pound (454 g) shrimp, peeled and deveined
- 2 ounces (57 g) Parmesan or Pecorino Romano cheese, grated
- 2 teaspoons lemon zest
- 4 ounces (113 g) fresh baby spinach

1. Bring the stock to a boil in a medium saucepan. Remove from the heat and set aside. 2. In a nonstick medium skillet over medium-high heat, heat the olive oil. Add the onion and sauté until tender, about 5 minutes. Add the garlic and sauté for 1 more minute. 3. Transfer the onion and garlic to the crock pot and add the artichoke hearts and barley. Season with some pepper. Stir in the seafood stock. 4. Cover and cook on high for 3 hours, or until the barley is tender and the liquid is just about

all absorbed. 5. About 15 minutes before the cooking time is completed, stir in the shrimp and grated cheese. Cover and continue to cook on high for another 10 minutes, or until the shrimp are opaque. 6. Add the lemon zest and fold in the baby spinach, stirring until it's wilted, about 1 minute. 7. Divide the risotto among the serving bowls and serve hot.

Seafood Laksa

Prep time: 30 minutes | Cook time: 2½ hours | Serves 6 to 8

- 2 tablespoons virgin coconut oil or extra-virgin olive oil
- 1 small onion, chopped
- 4 Thai bird chiles
- 1 (2-inch) piece fresh ginger, peeled and grated
- 1 (1-inch) piece fresh turmeric, peeled and grated
- 1 lemongrass stalk, tough outer leaves discarded, inner bulb chopped
- ¼ cup fresh cilantro
- 1 tablespoon tamarind paste
- ½ teaspoon ground cumin
- ½ teaspoon paprika
- 2 teaspoon coarse salt
- 2 cups unsweetened coconut milk
- 2 cups boiling water
- 4 kaffir lime leaves
- 2 teaspoon fish sauce
- 1 pound (454 g) medium shrimp, peeled and deveined (shells rinsed and reserved)
- 2 pounds (907 g) small mussels, scrubbed
- ¾ pound (340 g) firm fish fillet, such as halibut or cod, cut into 1-inch pieces
- 8 ounces (227 g) rice noodles
- Lime wedges, cubed firm tofu, sliced scallions, sliced Thai bird chiles, cilantro, and chili oil, for serving

1. Preheat a 7-quart crock pot. 2. Heat oil in a saucepan over medium. Add onion and cook until translucent, about 5 minutes. Add chiles, ginger, turmeric, lemongrass, cilantro, tamarind paste, cumin, paprika, and salt. Cook until fragrant, about 2 more minutes. Remove from heat and let cool. Transfer spice mixture to a food processor and puree to a thick paste. 3. Combine laksa paste, coconut milk, the boiling water, lime leaves, fish sauce, and shrimp shells in the crock pot. Cover and cook on low for 2 hours (we prefer this recipe on low). 4. Strain liquid through a medium sieve into a bowl, pressing down on solids; return broth to crock pot (discard solids). Add shrimp and mussels, and cook on low 20 minutes. Add fish and cook until shrimp is completely cooked through, fish is firm, and mussels open, about 10 minutes. 5. Meanwhile, prepare noodles according to package instructions. 6. To serve, divide noodles among bowls. Add broth and seafood, and top with tofu, scallions, chiles, and cilantro. Serve with lime wedges and chili oil.

Lemon-Dijon Salmon with Dill Barley

Prep time: 15 minutes | Cook time: 2 hours | Serves 6

- 1 medium yellow onion, diced
- 2 teaspoons garlic, minced
- 2 teaspoons olive oil
- 2 cups vegetable or chicken stock
- 1 cup quick-cooking barley
- 1 tablespoon minced fresh dill weed
- 1½ pounds (680 g) salmon
- fillets
- Sea salt
- Black pepper
- Lemon-Dijon Sauce:
- ⅓ cup Dijon mustard
- 3 tablespoons olive oil
- 3 tablespoons fresh lemon juice
- ⅓ cup plain Greek yogurt
- 1 clove garlic, minced

1. Combine the onion, garlic, and oil in a microwave-safe bowl. Heat in the microwave on 70 percent power for 4 to 5 minutes, stirring occasionally. Put into the crock pot. 2. Add the stock, barley, and dill weed to the crock pot and stir. 3. Season the salmon fillets with salt and pepper, and gently place them on top of the barley mixture. 4. Cover and cook on low for about 2 hours, until the salmon and barley are cooked through. Make the Lemon-Dijon Sauce: 5. In a small bowl, whisk together the Dijon mustard, olive oil, lemon juice, Greek yogurt, and garlic. Set aside and allow the flavors to blend. 6. To serve, place some barley on a plate and top with a salmon fillet. Spoon the lemon-Dijon sauce over the top of the salmon.

Low Country Seafood Boil

Prep time: 15 minutes | Cook time: 6 hours | Serves 8

- 8 medium red potatoes
- 2 large, sweet onions, such as Vidalia, quartered
- 2 pounds (907 g) smoked sausage, cut into 3-inch pieces
- 1 (3-ounce / 85-g) package seafood boil seasoning
- 1 (12-ounce / 340-g) bottle pale ale beer
- 10 cups water
- 4 ears of corn, halved
- 2 pounds (907 g) medium raw shrimp, shelled and deveined
- Cocktail sauce, for serving
- Hot sauce, for serving
- ½ cup melted butter, for serving
- 1 large lemon, cut into wedges, for garnish

1. In the crock pot, put the potatoes, onions, smoked sausage, seafood boil seasoning, beer, and water. Stir to combine. Cover and cook for 6 hours, or until the potatoes are tender when pierced with a fork. 2. About 45 minutes before serving, add the corn. Cover and continue cooking for 25 minutes. Add the shrimp, cover, and continue cooking until the shrimp are pink and no longer translucent. 3. Drain the crock pot, discard the cooking liquid, and serve the seafood with cocktail sauce, hot sauce, melted butter, and lemon wedges.

Cajun Shrimp

Prep time: 15 minutes | Cook time: 3½ to 7 hours | Serves 6

- ¾ pound (340 g) andouille sausage, cut into ½-inch rounds (you may substitute Kiel-basa if you cannot find andouille sausage)
- 1 red onion, sliced into wedges
- 2 garlic cloves, minced
- 2 celery stalks, coarsely chopped
- 1 red or green bell pepper, coarsely chopped
- 2 tablespoons all-purpose
- flour
- 1 (28-ounce / 794-g) can diced tomatoes, with their juice
- ¼ teaspoon cayenne pepper
- Coarse sea salt
- ½ pound (227 g) large shrimp, peeled and deveined
- 2 cups fresh okra, sliced (you may substitute frozen and thawed, if necessary)

1. Put the sausage, onion, garlic, celery, and bell pepper into the crock pot. Sprinkle with the flour and toss to coat. 2. Add the tomatoes and ½ cup water. Sprinkle with the cayenne pepper and season with salt. 3. Cover and cook on high for 3½ hours or on low for 7 hours, until the vegetables are tender. 4. Add the shrimp and okra. Cover and cook until the shrimp are opaque throughout, on high for 30 minutes or on low for 1 hour. Serve hot.

South-of-the-Border Halibut

Prep time: 10 minutes | Cook time: 3½ hours | Serves 6

- 3 cups prepared medium-hot salsa
- 2 tablespoons fresh lime juice
- 1 teaspoon ground cumin
- 2 to 3 pounds (907 g to 1.4
- kg) halibut fillets
- 1½ cup finely shredded Monterey Jack cheese (or Pepper Jack for a spicy topping)

1. Combine the salsa, lime juice, and cumin in the insert of a 5- to 7-quart crock pot and stir. Cover the crock pot and cook on low for 2 hours. 2. Put the halibut in the cooker and spoon some of the sauce over the top of the fish. Sprinkle the cheese evenly over the fish. Cover and cook for an additional 30 to 45 minutes. 3. Remove the halibut from the crock pot and serve on a bed of the sauce.

Citrus Swordfish

Prep time: 15 minutes | Cook time: 1½ hours | Serves 2

- Nonstick cooking oil spray
- 1½ pounds (680 g) swordfish fillets
- Sea salt
- Black pepper
- 1 yellow onion, chopped
- 5 tablespoons chopped fresh flat-leaf parsley
- 1 tablespoon olive oil
- 2 teaspoons lemon zest
- 2 teaspoons orange zest
- Orange and lemon slices, for garnish
- Fresh parsley sprigs, for garnish

1. Coat the interior of the crock pot crock with nonstick cooking oil spray. 2. Season the fish fillets with salt and pepper. Place the fish in the crock pot. 3. Distribute the onion, parsley, olive oil, lemon zest, and orange zest over fish. 4. Cover and cook on low for 1½ hours. 5. Serve hot, garnished with orange and lemon slices and sprigs of fresh parsley.

Sea Bass Tagine

Prep time: 25 minutes | Cook time: 6 to 7½ hours | Serves 6

- 2 pounds (907 g) sea bass fillets
- ½ cup olive oil
- Grated zest of 1 lemon
- ¼ cup lemon juice
- 1 teaspoon sweet paprika
- ½ cup finely chopped fresh cilantro
- 2 cloves garlic, chopped
- 1 medium onion, finely chopped
- 1 teaspoon ground cumin
- ½ teaspoon saffron threads, crushed
- 1 (28- to 32-ounce / 794- to 907-g) can crushed tomatoes, with their juice
- 6 medium Yukon gold potatoes, quartered
- 1 teaspoon salt
- ½ teaspoon freshly ground black pepper
- ½ cup finely chopped fresh Italian parsley

1. Place the fish in a zipper-top plastic bag. 2. Whisk ¼ cup of the oil, the zest, lemon juice, paprika, and cilantro together in a small bowl. Pour the marinade over the fish in the bag. Seal the bag and refrigerate for at least 1 hour or up to 4 hours. 3. Heat the remaining ¼ cup oil in a large skillet over medium-high heat. Add the garlic, onion, cumin, and saffron and sauté until the onion is softened, 5 to 7 minutes. 4. Add the tomatoes and stir to combine. Place the potatoes in the bottom of the insert of a 5- to 7-quart crock pot and sprinkle them evenly with the salt and pepper, tossing to coat. Add the tomato mixture to the insert. Cover and cook on low for 5 to 6 hours, until the potatoes are almost tender. 5. Pour the marinade into the insert and stir the potatoes and sauce to combine. Put the fish on top of the potatoes and spoon some of the sauce over the top. Cook for an additional 1 to 1½ hours, until the sea bass is cooked through and is opaque in the center. 6. Sprinkle the parsley evenly over the top of the sea bass and serve immediately, scooping up some potatoes and sauce with the fish.

Acadiana Shrimp Barbecue

Prep time: 15 minutes | Cook time: 4 hours | Serves 6 to 8

- 1 cup (2 sticks) unsalted butter
- ¼ cup olive oil
- 8 cloves garlic, sliced
- 2 teaspoons dried oregano
- 1 teaspoon dried thyme
- ½ teaspoon freshly ground black pepper
- Pinch of cayenne pepper
- 2 teaspoons sweet paprika
- ¼ cup Worcestershire sauce
- ¼ cup lemon juice
- 3 pounds (1.4 kg) large shrimp, peeled and deveined
- ½ cup finely chopped fresh Italian parsley

1. Put the butter, oil, garlic, oregano, thyme, pepper, cayenne, paprika, Worcestershire, and lemon juice in the insert of a 5- to 7-quart crock pot. Cover and cook on low for 4 hours. 2. Turn the cooker up to high and add the shrimp, tossing them in the butter sauce. Cover and cook for an additional 10 to 5 minutes, until the shrimp are pink. 3. Transfer the shrimp from the crock pot to a large serving bowl and pour the sauce over the shrimp. Sprinkle with the parsley and serve.

Lemon, Garlic, and Butter Halibut

Prep time: 15 minutes | Cook time: 5 hours | Serves 6

- 1 cup (2 sticks) unsalted butter
- ½ cup olive oil
- 6 cloves garlic, sliced
- 1 teaspoon sweet paprika
- ½ cup lemon juice
- Grated zest of 1 lemon
- ¼ cup finely chopped fresh chives
- 2 to 3 pounds (907 g to 1.4 kg) halibut fillets
- ½ cup finely chopped fresh Italian parsley

1. Combine the butter, oil, garlic, paprika, lemon juice, zest, and chives in the insert of a 5- to 7-quart crock pot and stir to combine. Cover and cook on low for 4 hours. 2. Add the halibut to the pot, spooning the sauce over the halibut. Cover and cook for an additional 40 minutes, until the halibut is cooked through and opaque. 3. Sprinkle the parsley evenly over the fish, and serve immediately.

Poached Salmon Cakes in White Wine Butter Sauce

Prep time: 15 minutes | Cook time: 5 hours | Serves 6

* White Wine Butter Sauce:
* ½ cup (1 stick) unsalted butter
* 1 teaspoon Old Bay seasoning
* 2 cloves garlic, sliced
* 2 ½ cups white wine or vermouth
* Salmon Cakes:
* 4 cups cooked salmon, flaked
* 1 (6-ounce / 170-g) jar marinated artichoke hearts, drained and coarsely chopped
* 1 cup fresh bread crumbs
* ½ cup freshly grated Parmigiano-Reggiano cheese
* 1 large egg, beaten
* ½ teaspoon freshly ground black pepper

1. Put all the sauce ingredients in the insert of a 5- to 7-quart crock pot and stir to combine. Cover and cook on low for 4 hours. 2. Put all the salmon cake ingredients in a large mixing bowl and stir to combine. Form the mixture into 2-inch cakes. Place the cakes in the simmering sauce and spoon the sauce over the cakes. 3. Cover and cook for an additional 1 hour, until the cakes are tender. Carefully remove the cakes to a serving platter. 4. Strain the sauce through a fine-mesh sieve into a saucepan. Bring the sauce to a boil and reduce by half. 5. Serve the sauce over the cakes, or serve on the side.

Miso-Glazed Cod

Prep time: 15 minutes | Cook time: 5 hours | Serves 6

* ½ cup white miso paste
* ¼ cup rice wine (mirin)
* ¼ firmly packed light brown sugar
* 1 teaspoon rice vinegar
* 1 ½ cups water
* 2 pounds (907 g) black cod (if unavailable, use fresh
* cod, halibut, sea bass, or salmon)
* 6 green onions, finely chopped, using the white and tender green parts
* ¼ cup toasted sesame seeds for garnish

1. Combine the miso, rice wine, sugar, rice vinegar, and water in the insert of a 5- to 7-quart crock pot. 2. Cover and cook on low for 4 hours. Add the cod, spooning the sauce over the top. Cover and cook for an additional 30 to 45 minutes. 3. Remove the cod from the slow-cooker insert and cover with aluminum foil to keep warm. Pour the sauce in a saucepan. Bring to a boil and reduce by half until it begins to look syrupy, about 15 to 20 minutes. Add the green onions to the sauce. 4. Serve each piece of cod in a pool of the sauce, and sprinkle each serving with sesame seeds. Serve any additional sauce on the side.

Catalan-Style Seafood Stew

Prep time: 20 minutes | Cook time: 7 hours | Serves 6 to 8

* ½ cup extra-virgin olive oil
* 2 medium onions, finely chopped
* 2 medium red bell peppers, seeded and finely chopped
* 6 cloves garlic, minced
* 1 teaspoon saffron threads, crushed
* 1 teaspoon hot paprika
* 1 cup finely chopped Spanish chorizo or soppressata salami
* 1 (28- to 32-ounce / 794-
* to 907-g) can crushed tomatoes
* 2 cups clam juice
* 1 cup chicken broth
* 2 pounds (907 g) firm-fleshed fish, such as halibut, monkfish, cod, or sea bass fillets, cut into 1-inch chunks
* 1½ pounds (680 g) littleneck clams
* ½ cup finely chopped fresh Italian parsley

1. Heat the oil in a large skillet over medium-high heat. Add the onions, bell peppers, garlic, saffron, paprika, and chorizo and sauté until the vegetables are softened, 5 to 7 minutes. Add the tomatoes and transfer the contents of the skillet to the insert of a 5- to 7-quart crock pot. Add the clam juice and broth and stir to combine. 2. Cover and cook on low for 6 hours. Add the fish and clams to the slow-cooker insert, spooning some of the sauce over the fish and pushing the clams under the sauce. 3. Cover and cook for an additional 45 to 50 minutes, until the clams have opened and the fish is cooked through and opaque. Discard any clams that haven't opened. 4. Sprinkle the parsley over the stew and serve immediately.

Garlic Crab Claws

Prep time: 10 minutes | Cook time: 5½ hours | Serves 6 to 8

* 1 cup (2 sticks) unsalted butter
* ½ cup olive oil
* 10 cloves garlic, sliced
* 2 tablespoons Old Bay seasoning
* 2 cups dry white wine or vermouth
* 1 lemon, thinly sliced
* 3 to 4 pounds (1.4 to 1.8 kg) cooked crab legs and claws, cracked

1. Put the butter, oil, garlic, seasoning, wine, and lemon in the insert of a 5- to 7-quart crock pot. 2. Cover and cook on low for 4 hours. Add the crab, spoon the sauce over the crab, and cook for an additional 1½ hours, turning the crab in the sauce during cooking. 3. Serve the crab from the cooker set on warm.

Potato-Crusted Sea Bass

Prep time: 15 minutes | Cook time: 1½ hours | Serves 6

- 1 cup (2 sticks) unsalted butter, melted and cooled
- ½ cup fresh lemon juice
- Grated zest of 1 lemon
- 2 cloves garlic, minced
- 8 tablespoons olive oil
- 2 tablespoons Old Bay seasoning
- 2 to 3 pounds (907 g to 1.4 kg) sea bass fillets, cut to fit the slow-cooker insert
- 6 medium Yukon gold potatoes, cut into ¼-inch-thick slices

1. Stir the butter, lemon juice, zest, garlic, and 2 tablespoons of the olive oil together in a small bowl. Combine the remaining 6 tablespoons oil and the seasoning in a large mixing bowl. 2. Paint the sea bass with some of the butter sauce and set aside. Toss the potatoes in the seasoned oil. Pour half the butter sauce in the insert of a 5- to 7-quart crock pot. 3. Place half the potatoes in the bottom of the crock pot. Place the sea bass on top of the potatoes and pour half the remaining butter sauce over the sea bass. Place the remaining potatoes on top of the sea bass and drizzle with the remaining butter sauce. 4. Cover and cook on high for 1½ hours, until the potatoes begin to turn golden and the sea bass is cooked through and opaque in the middle. Remove the cover and cook for an additional 15 to 20 minutes. 5. Serve immediately.

Moroccan Sea Bass

Prep time: 20 minutes | Cook time: 3 to 4 hours | Serves 8

- 2 tablespoons extra-virgin olive oil
- 1 large yellow onion, finely chopped
- 1 medium red bell pepper, cut into ½-inch strips
- 1 medium yellow bell pepper, cut into ½-inch strips
- 4 garlic cloves, minced
- 1 teaspoon saffron threads, crushed in the palm of your hand
- 1½ teaspoons sweet paprika
- ¼ teaspoon hot paprika or ¼ teaspoon smoked paprika
- (or pimentón)
- ½ teaspoon ground ginger
- 1 (15-ounce / 425-g) can diced tomatoes, with the juice
- ¼ cup fresh orange juice
- 2 pounds (907 g) fresh sea bass fillets
- ¼ cup finely chopped fresh flat-leaf parsley
- ¼ cup finely chopped fresh cilantro
- Sea salt
- Black pepper
- 1 navel orange, thinly sliced, for garnish

1. In a large skillet, heat the olive oil over medium-high heat. Add the onion, red and yellow bell peppers, garlic, saffron, sweet paprika, hot or smoked paprika, and ginger and cook, stirring often, for 3 minutes, or until the onion begins to soften. 2. Add the tomatoes and stir for another 2 minutes, to blend the flavors. 3. Transfer the mixture to the crock pot and stir in the orange juice. 4. Place the sea bass fillets on top of the tomato mixture, and spoon some of the mixture over the fish. Cover and cook on high for 2 hours, or on low for 3 to 4 hours. At the end of the cooking time, the sea bass should be opaque in the center. 5. Carefully lift the fish out of the crock pot with a spatula and transfer to a serving platter. Cover loosely with aluminum foil. 6. Skim off any excess fat from the sauce, stir in the parsley and cilantro, and season with salt and pepper. 7. Spoon some of the sauce over the fish, and garnish with the orange slices. Serve hot, passing the remaining sauce on the side.

Seafood Stew

Prep time: 15 minutes | Cook time: 6 hours | Serves 8

- 1 pound (454 g) waxy baby potatoes, such as Yukon Gold
- 2 medium onions, finely chopped
- 2 celery stalks, finely chopped
- 5 garlic cloves, minced
- 1 (28-ounce / 794-g) can crushed tomatoes
- 1 (8-ounce / 227-g) bottle clam juice
- 8 ounces (227 g) low-sodium fish stock
- 1 (6-ounce / 170-g) can tomato paste
- 1 tablespoon balsamic vinegar
- 1 teaspoon sugar
- ½ teaspoon celery salt
- ½ teaspoon kosher salt, plus more for seasoning
- ½ teaspoon freshly ground black pepper, plus more for seasoning
- 2 bay leaves
- 1 pound (454 g) firm-fleshed white fish, such as cod, cut into 1-inch pieces
- ½ pound (227 g) medium uncooked shrimp, shelled and deveined
- ½ pound (227 g) scallops, small side muscle removed, halved
- ¼ cup finely chopped flat-leaf parsley, for garnish

1. To the crock pot, add the potatoes, onions, celery, garlic, tomatoes, clam juice, fish stock, tomato paste, vinegar, sugar, celery salt, kosher salt, pepper, and bay leaves. Stir to combine. Cover and cook on low for 6 hours, or until the potatoes are tender when pierced with a fork. 2. About 30 minutes before serving, add the white fish, shrimp, and scallops. Cover and continue cooking on low until cooked through. 3. Discard the bay leaves. Season with additional salt and pepper, as needed. Ladle the stew into bowls, garnish with the parsley, and serve immediately.

Creole Crayfish

Prep time: 15 minutes | Cook time: 3 to 8 hours | Serves 2

- 1½ cups diced celery
- 1 large yellow onion, chopped
- 2 small bell peppers, any colors, chopped
- 1 (8-ounce / 227-g) can tomato sauce
- 1 (28-ounce / 794-g) can whole tomatoes, broken up, with the juice
- 1 clove garlic, minced
- 1 teaspoon sea salt
- ¼ teaspoon black pepper
- 6 drops hot pepper sauce (like Tabasco)
- 1 pound (454 g) precooked crayfish meat

1. Place the celery, onion, and bell peppers in the crock pot. Add the tomato sauce, tomatoes, and garlic. Sprinkle with the salt and pepper and add the hot sauce. 2. Cover and cook on high for 3 to 4 hours or on low for 6 to 8 hours. 3. About 30 minutes before the cooking time is completed, add the crayfish. 4. Serve hot.

Scallop and Crab Cioppino

Prep time: 15 minutes | Cook time: 7 hours | Serves 4

- Cooking oil spray
- 1 medium yellow onion, finely chopped
- 4 cloves garlic, minced
- 1 (15-ounce / 425-g) can diced tomatoes, with the juice
- 1 (10-ounce / 283-g) can diced tomatoes with green chiles
- 2 cups seafood stock
- 1 cup red wine
- 3 tablespoons chopped fresh basil
- 2 bay leaves
- 1 pound (454 g) cooked crab meat, shredded
- 1½ pounds (680 g) scallops
- Sea salt
- Black pepper
- ¼ cup fresh flat-leaf parsley, for garnish

1. Coat a large sauté pan with cooking oil spray and heat over medium-high heat. Add the onion and sauté for about 5 minutes, until softened. 2. Add the garlic and sauté until golden and fragrant, about 2 minutes. 3. Transfer the onion and garlic to the crock pot, and add the tomatoes, tomatoes with green chiles, stock, wine, basil, and bay leaves. Cover and cook on low for 6 hours. 4. About 30 minutes before the cooking time is completed, add the crab meat and scallops. Cover and cook on high for 30 minutes. The seafood will turn opaque. Season to taste with salt and pepper. Serve hot, garnished with parsley.

Chapter ⑥

Stews and Soups

Spicy Lentil and Chickpea Stew

Prep time: 25 minutes | Cook time: 8 hours | Serves 8

- 2 teaspoons olive oil
- 1 medium onion, thinly sliced
- 1 teaspoon dried oregano
- ½ teaspoon crushed red pepper flakes
- 2 (15-ounce / 425-g) cans chickpeas or garbanzo beans, rinsed and drained
- 1 cup dried lentils, rinsed
- 1 (2¼-ounce / 64-g) can sliced ripe olives, drained
- 3 teaspoons smoked paprika
- 4 cups vegetable broth
- 4 (8-ounce / 227-g) cans no-salt-added tomato sauce
- 4 cups fresh baby spinach
- ¾ cup fat-free plain yogurt

1. In a small skillet, heat oil over medium-high heat. Add onion, oregano and pepper flakes; cook and stir 8 to 10 minutes or until onion is tender. Transfer to a 5- or 6-quart crock pot. 2. Add chickpeas, lentils, olives and paprika; stir in broth and tomato sauce. Cook, covered, on low 8 to 10 hours or until lentils are tender. Stir in spinach. Top with yogurt.

Pacific Rim Pork and Noodle Soup

Prep time: 25 minutes | Cook time: 5 to 6 hours | Serves 8

- ½ cup soy sauce
- ¼ cup hoisin sauce
- ¼ cup rice wine
- Pinch five-spice powder
- 2 tablespoons toasted sesame oil
- 1 pork tenderloin (1¼ to 1½ pounds / 567 to 680 g), silver skin removed, cut into ½-inch slices
- 2 tablespoons vegetable oil
- 2 teaspoons freshly grated ginger
- 2 cloves garlic, minced
- 1 medium onion, coarsely chopped
- 1 bunch bok choy, cut into 1-inch pieces
- 2 medium carrots, cut into julienne strips
- 8 cups beef broth
- 8 ounces (227 g) fresh soba noodles, or 12 ounces (340 g) dried
- 4 green onions, finely chopped, using the white and tender green parts
- ¼ cup toasted sesame seeds, for garnish

1. Whisk together the soy sauce, hoisin, rice wine, five-spice powder, and sesame oil in a large glass bowl. Add the pork, cover, and refrigerate for at least 1 hour and up to 8 hours. 2. Heat the vegetable oil in a large skillet or wok over high heat. Remove the pork from the marinade and add to the skillet. Stir-fry, a few pieces at a time, until the pork begins to color, 3 to 4 minutes. 3. Transfer the pork to the insert of a 5- to 7-quart crock pot. Add the ginger and garlic to the same skillet and stir-fry for 1 minute, until fragrant. Add the onion, bok choy, and carrots and stir-fry until the vegetables are softened, 3 to 4 minutes. Deglaze the skillet with 1 cup of the broth, scraping up any browned bits from the bottom of the pan. 4. Transfer the contents of the skillet to the slow-cooker insert. Add the remaining 7 cups broth to the slow-cooker insert. Cover and cook on low for 4 to 5 hours, until the pork and vegetables are tender. Add the noodles and green onions. Cover and cook for an additional 45 minutes. 5. Serve the soup garnished with the toasted sesame seeds.

Broccoli-Cheese Soup

Prep time: 10 minutes | Cook time: 8 to 10 hours | Serves 8

- 2 (16-ounce / 454-g) packages frozen chopped broccoli
- 2 (10¾-ounce / 305-g) cans Cheddar cheese soup
- 2 (12-ounce / 340-g) cans evaporated milk
- ¼ cup finely chopped onions
- ½ teaspoon seasoned salt
- ¼ teaspoon pepper
- Sunflower seeds (optional)
- Crumbled bacon (optional)

1. Combine all ingredients except sunflower seeds and bacon in crock pot. 2. Cover. Cook on low 8 to 10 hours. 3. Garnish with sunflower seeds and bacon.

Bean and Herb Soup

Prep time: 45 minutes | Cook time: 1 hour | Serves 6 to 8

- 1½ cups dry mixed beans
- 5 cups water
- 1 ham hock
- 1 cup chopped onions
- 1 cup chopped celery
- 1 cup chopped carrots
- 2 to 3 cups water
- 1 teaspoon salt
- ¼ to ½ teaspoon pepper
- 1 to 2 teaspoons fresh basil, or ½ teaspoon dried basil
- 1 to 2 teaspoons fresh oregano, or ½ teaspoon dried oregano
- 1 to 2 teaspoons fresh thyme, or ½ teaspoon dried thyme
- 2 cups fresh tomatoes, crushed, or 1 (14½-ounce / 411-g) can crushed tomatoes

1. Combine beans, water, and ham in saucepan. Bring to boil. Turn off heat and let stand 1 hour. 2. Combine onions, celery, and carrots in 2 to 3 cups water in another saucepan. Cook until soft. Mash slightly. 3. Combine all ingredients in crock pot. 4. Cover. Cook on high 2 hours, and then on low 2 hours.

Sausage Fennel Minestrone

Prep time: 15 minutes | Cook time: 4 hours | Serves 6

- 6 cups chicken stock
- 2 tablespoons tomato paste
- 1 large yellow onion, chopped
- 1 cup diced fennel
- ½ cup chopped celery
- 1 (15-ounce / 425-g) can cannellini beans
- 1 (28-ounce / 794-g) can diced tomatoes with the
- juice
- ½ teaspoon sea salt
- 1 bay leaf
- ½ teaspoon dried thyme
- 1 pound (454 g) hot Italian sausage, casings removed
- 2 cups cooked orecchiette pasta
- 2 cups stemmed, chopped kale or Swiss chard

1. In the crock pot, combine the chicken stock, tomato paste, onion, fennel, celery, cannellini, and tomatoes. Add ½ teaspoon salt and the bay leaf and thyme. 2. In a nonstick medium skillet over medium-high heat, sauté the sausage, breaking it up into small chunks, until browned, about 5 minutes. Drain on a paper towel–lined plate. 3. Add the browned sausage to the crock pot. Cover and cook on high for 4 hours. 4. Stir in the orecchiette and kale, and cook until heated through, about 5 minutes. Serve hot.

Vegetable Soup Provençal

Prep time: 20 minutes | Cook time: 2 to 4 hours | Serves 8

- Soup:
- 2 tablespoons extra-virgin olive oil
- 3 leeks (white and tender green parts), halved lengthwise, cleaned, and cut crosswise into ½-inch half-moons
- 3 ribs celery, coarsely chopped
- 3 medium carrots, coarsely chopped
- 2 teaspoons herbs de Provence
- ½ cup dry white wine
- 1 (15-ounce / 425-g) can diced tomatoes with the juice
- 8 cups chicken or vegetable stock
- 2 medium zucchini, cut into ½-inch chunks
- 2 cups fresh or frozen, thawed peas
- 1 head escarole, cut into 1-inch pieces
- 2 (15-ounce / 425-g) cans small white beans, drained and rinsed
- Pistou:
- 2 cups firmly packed fresh basil leaves
- 6 garlic cloves, peeled
- ½ cup extra-virgin olive oil
- Sea salt
- Black pepper

Make the Soup: 1. In a large skillet, heat the olive oil over medium-high heat. Add the leeks, celery, carrots, and herbs de Provence and sauté until the carrots begin to soften, about 3 minutes. 2. Add the wine, and cook to allow the wine to evaporate a bit, about 2 minutes. Transfer the contents of the skillet to the crock pot. 3. Add the tomatoes, stock, zucchini, peas, escarole, and beans to the crock pot and stir to combine. Cover and cook on high for 2 hours or on low for 4 hours. Make the Pistou: 4. In a blender or food processor, combine the basil and garlic and pulse to break them up. 5. With the machine running, add ¼ cup of the olive oil. 6. Scrape down the sides of the blender. Season with salt and black pepper, if necessary. 7. If the pistou is very thick, add more olive oil, 1 to 2 teaspoons at a time. The pistou should hold together and not be runny. 8. Transfer the pistou to an airtight glass jar, and float the remaining olive oil on the top to prevent the basil from discoloring. 9. When ready to serve, season with salt and pepper, as necessary. Ladle the hot soup into bowls, and add 1 to 2 dollops of pistou onto the center of each serving.

Tempting Beef Stew

Prep time: 10 minutes | Cook time: 10 to 12 hours | Serves 10 to 12

- 2 to 3 pounds (907 g to 1.4 kg) beef stewing meat
- 3 carrots, thinly sliced
- 1 (1-pound / 454-g) package frozen green peas with onions
- 1 (1-pound / 454-g) package frozen green beans
- 1 (16-ounce / 454-g) can
- whole or stewed tomatoes
- ½ cup beef broth
- ½ cup white wine
- ½ cup brown sugar
- 4 tablespoons tapioca
- ½ cup bread crumbs
- 2 teaspoons salt
- 1 bay leaf
- Pepper to taste

1. Combine all ingredients in crock pot. 2. Cover. Cook on low 10 to 12 hours. 3. Serve.

Joy's Brunswick Stew

Prep time: 10 minutes | Cook time: 4 hours | Serves 8

- 1 pound (454 g) skinless, boneless chicken breasts, cubed
- 2 potatoes, thinly sliced
- 1 (10¾-ounce / 305-g) can tomato soup
- 1 (16-ounce / 454-g) can stewed tomatoes
- 1 (10-ounce / 283-g) package frozen corn
- 1 (10-ounce / 283-g) package frozen lima beans
- 3 tablespoons onion flakes
- ¼ teaspoon salt
- ⅛ teaspoon pepper

1. Combine all ingredients in crock pot. 2. Cover. Cook on high 2 hours. Reduce to low and cook 2 hours.

Southwest Corn Soup

Prep time: 10 minutes | Cook time: 4 hours | Serves 6

- 2 (4-ounce / 113-g) cans chopped green chilies, undrained
- 2 small zucchini, cut into bite-sized pieces
- 1 medium onion, thinly sliced
- 3 cloves garlic, minced
- 1 teaspoon ground cumin
- 3 (14½-ounce / 411-g) cans fat-free, sodium-reduced
- chicken broth
- 1½ to 2 cups cooked turkey, shredded
- 1 (15-ounce / 425-g) can chickpeas or black beans, rinsed and drained
- 1 (10-ounce / 283-g) package frozen corn
- 1 teaspoon dried oregano
- ½ cup chopped cilantro

1. Combine all ingredients in crock pot. 2. Cook on low 4 hours.

Sopranos-Style Sausage Minestrone

Prep time: 30 minutes | Cook time: 8 to 10 hours | Serves 8

- 1½ pounds (680 g) sweet Italian sausage, bulk or removed from casing
- 2 tablespoons extra-virgin olive oil
- 4 slices prosciutto, cut into julienne strips
- 2 medium onions, coarsely chopped
- 4 medium carrots, coarsely chopped
- 4 stalks celery with leaves, coarsely chopped
- 2 teaspoons finely chopped fresh rosemary
- ½ cup medium- to full-bodied red wine
- 1 (15-ounce / 425-g) can crushed plum tomatoes,
- with their juice
- 4 medium red potatoes, cut into ½-inch dice
- 4 ounces (113 g) green beans, ends snipped, cut into 1-inch lengths
- 2 medium zucchini, cut into ½-inch half rounds
- 1 cup dried brown lentils or split peas
- 1 head escarole or Swiss chard, cut into 1-inch pieces
- Rind from Parmigiano-Reggiano cheese, cut into ½-inch pieces (optional)
- 8 cups beef broth
- 2 cups cooked orzo

1. Cook the sausage in a large skillet over high heat, breaking up any large pieces, until it is no longer pink. 2. Transfer the sausage to the insert of a 5- to 7-quart crock pot. Remove all but 2 tablespoons of fat from the pan and add the olive oil. Add the prosciutto and sauté for 2 minutes, until it begins to get crisp. 3. Add the onions, carrots, celery, and rosemary and sauté until the onions begin to soften, about 5 minutes. Deglaze the pan with the wine and boil until the wine is reduced by half, about 3 minutes. Add the tomatoes and cook for 2 minutes. 4. Transfer the contents of the skillet to the slow-cooker insert and stir in the potatoes, beans, zucchini, lentils, escarole, cheese rind (if using), and broth. Cover and cook on low for 8 to 10 hours, until the soup is thickened and the lentils are softened. 5. Stir in the orzo and serve.

Green Bean and Sausage Soup

Prep time: 25 minutes | Cook time: 7 to 10 hours | Serves 5 to 6

- 1 medium onion, chopped
- 2 carrots, sliced
- 2 ribs celery, sliced
- 1 tablespoon olive oil
- 5 medium potatoes, cubed
- 1 (10-ounce / 283-g) package frozen green beans
- 2 (14½-ounce / 411-g) cans chicken broth
- 2 broth cans water
- ⅓ pound (151 g) link
- sausage, sliced, or bulk sausage, browned
- 2 tablespoons chopped fresh parsley, or 2 teaspoons dried
- 1 to 2 tablespoons chopped fresh oregano, or 1 to 2 teaspoons dried
- 1 teaspoon Italian spice
- Salt to taste
- Pepper to taste

1. Sauté onion, carrots, and celery in oil in skillet until tender. 2. Combine all ingredients in crock pot. 3. Cover. Cook on high 1 to 2 hours and then on low 6 to 8 hours. 4. Serve.

Faux Lasagna Soup

Prep time: 20 minutes | Cook time: 6 hours | Serves 6

- 3 tablespoons extra-virgin olive oil, divided
- 1 pound (454 g) ground beef
- ½ sweet onion, chopped
- 2 teaspoons minced garlic
- 4 cups beef broth
- 1 (28-ounce / 794-g) can
- diced tomatoes, undrained
- 1 zucchini, diced
- 1½ tablespoons dried basil
- 2 teaspoons dried oregano
- 4 ounces (113 g) cream cheese
- 1 cup shredded Mozzarella

1. Lightly grease the insert of the crock pot with 1 tablespoon of the olive oil. 2. In a large skillet over medium-high heat, heat the remaining 2 tablespoons of the olive oil. Add the ground beef and sauté until it is cooked through, about 6 minutes. 3. Add the onion and garlic and sauté for an additional 3 minutes. 4. Transfer the meat mixture to the insert. 5. Stir in the broth, tomatoes, zucchini, basil, and oregano. 6. Cover and cook on low for 6 hours. 7. Stir in the cream cheese and Mozzarella and serve.

Corn Chowder

Prep time: 15 minutes | Cook time: 6 to 7 hours | Serves 4

- 6 slices bacon, diced
- ½ cup chopped onions
- 2 cups diced peeled potatoes
- 2 (10-ounce / 283-g) packages frozen corn
- 1 (16-ounce / 454-g) can

- cream-style corn
- 1 tablespoon sugar
- 1 teaspoon Worcestershire sauce
- 1 teaspoon seasoned salt
- ¼ teaspoon pepper
- 1 cup water

1. In skillet, brown bacon until crisp. Remove bacon, reserving drippings. 2. Add onions and potatoes to skillet and sauté for 5 minutes. Drain. 3. Combine all ingredients in crock pot. Mix well. 4. Cover. Cook on low 6 to 7 hours.

Chicken-Bacon Soup

Prep time: 15 minutes | Cook time: 8 hours | Serves 8

- 1 tablespoon extra-virgin olive oil
- 6 cups chicken broth
- 3 cups cooked chicken, chopped
- 1 sweet onion, chopped
- 2 celery stalks, chopped
- 1 carrot, diced

- 2 teaspoons minced garlic
- 1½ cups heavy (whipping) cream
- 1 cup cream cheese
- 1 cup cooked chopped bacon
- 1 tablespoon chopped fresh parsley, for garnish

1. Lightly grease the insert of the crock pot with the olive oil. 2. Add the broth, chicken, onion, celery, carrot, and garlic. 3. Cover and cook on low for 8 hours. 4. Stir in the heavy cream, cream cheese, and bacon. 5. Serve topped with the parsley.

Wild Rice Soup

Prep time: 15 minutes | Cook time: 4 to 6 hours | Serves 8

- 2 tablespoons butter
- ½ cup dry wild rice
- 6 cups fat-free, low-sodium chicken stock
- ½ cup minced onions
- ½ cup minced celery
- ½ pound (227 g) winter

- squash, peeled, seeded, cut in ½-inch cubes
- 2 cups cooked chicken, chopped
- ½ cup browned, slivered almonds

1. Melt butter in small skillet. Add rice and sauté for 10 minutes over low heat. Transfer to crock pot. 2. Add all remaining ingredients except chicken and almonds. 3. Cover. Cook on low 4 to 6 hours. One hour before serving stir in chicken. 4. Top with browned slivered almonds just before serving.

Cajun Corn and Crab Soup

Prep time: 15 minutes | Cook time: 2½ hours | Serves 8

- ½ cup (1 stick) unsalted butter
- 2 medium sweet onions, such as Vidalia, finely chopped
- 4 stalks celery, finely chopped
- ½ teaspoon sweet paprika
- ¼ teaspoon freshly ground black pepper
- ⅛ teaspoon cayenne pepper
- ½ teaspoon dried thyme
- 3 tablespoons all-purpose

- flour
- 5 cups seafood stock
- 1 (16-ounce / 454-g) package frozen white corn, defrosted
- 1 pound (454 g) lump crab meat, picked over for cartilage and shells
- 1 cup cream
- Salt and freshly ground black pepper
- ½ cup finely chopped fresh chives

1. Melt the butter in a saucepan over medium-high heat. 2. Add the onions, celery, paprika, black and cayenne peppers, and thyme and sauté until the vegetables are softened, 3 to 5 minutes. Stir in the flour and cook for 3 minutes, whisking the roux constantly. Stir in the stock and bring the mixture to a boil. 3. Transfer the contents of the skillet to the insert of a 5- to 7-quart crock pot. Add the corn, cover, and cook on high for 2 hours. Stir in the crab meat and cream and cook on low for an additional 30 minutes. 4. Season with salt and pepper. Garnish each serving with chives.

Beef Barley Stew

Prep time: 15 minutes | Cook time: 9 to 10 hours | Serves 6

- ½ pound (227 g) lean round steak, cut in ½-inch cubes
- 4 carrots, peeled and cut in ¼-inch slices
- 1 cup chopped yellow onions
- ½ cup coarsely chopped green bell peppers
- 1 clove garlic, pressed
- ½ pound (227 g) fresh button mushrooms,

- quartered
- ¾ cup dry pearl barley
- ½ teaspoon salt
- ¼ teaspoon ground black pepper
- ½ teaspoon dried thyme
- ½ teaspoon dried sweet basil
- 1 bay leaf
- 5 cups fat-free, low-sodium beef broth

1. Combine all ingredients in crock pot. 2. Cover. Cook on low 9 to 10 hours.

New England Fish Chowder

Prep time: 25 minutes | Cook time: 3½ to 4 hours | Serves 8

* 8 strips thick-cut bacon, cut into ½-inch pieces
* 1 large onion, finely chopped
* 4 stalks celery, finely chopped
* 1 teaspoon dried thyme
* 3 tablespoons all-purpose flour
* 3 cups chicken broth
* 2 (8-ounce / 227-g) bottles clam juice
* 5 medium red or Yukon gold potatoes, cut into ½-inch chunks
* 1 bay leaf
* 1½ pounds (680 g) thick-fleshed fish, such as sea bass, halibut, haddock, or cod, cut into 2-inch cubes
* 1½ cups heavy cream
* ¼ cup finely chopped fresh Italian parsley, for garnish
* ¼ cup finely chopped fresh chives, for garnish

1. Cook the bacon in a large skillet over medium-high heat until crisp and remove it to paper towels to drain. Remove all but ¼ cup of the bacon drippings from the skillet. 2. Add the onion, celery, and thyme and sauté until the onion is translucent, 5 to 7 minutes. Stir in the flour and cook for 3 minutes, whisking the roux constantly. Gradually stir in the broth and clam juice and bring to a boil. 3. Transfer the contents of the skillet to the insert of a 5- to 7-quart crock pot. Add the potatoes and bay leaf. Cover and cook on high for 2½ to 3 hours, until the potatoes are tender. 4. Stir in the bacon, fish, and cream. Cover and cook for an additional 45 minutes to 1 hour, until the fish is cooked through. 5. Remove the bay leaf and serve the chowder garnished with the parsley and chives.

Moroccan Lamb Stew

Prep time: 20 minutes | Cook time: 8 hours | Serves 2

* ¾ pound (340 g) cubed lamb shoulder, trimmed of fat
* 1 teaspoon ground coriander
* ½ teaspoon ground cumin
* ½ teaspoon salt
* ¼ teaspoon ground cinnamon
* ⅛ teaspoon freshly ground black pepper
* 1 cup sliced fennel
* 1 carrot, sliced
* 2 garlic cloves, minced
* 1 (15 ounces / 425 g) can chickpeas, rinsed and drained
* ½ cup golden raisins
* 1 large tomato, seeded and chopped
* 1½ cups chicken stock

1. In a medium bowl, sprinkle the lamb shoulder with the coriander, cumin, salt, cinnamon, and pepper, and rub the spices into the meat. 2. In the crock pot, combine the lamb with the remaining ingredients and stir. 3. Cover and cook on low for 8 hours, or until the lamb is very tender. 4. Ladle the stew into 2 bowls and serve.

Vegetarian Soup

Prep time: 10 minutes | Cook time: 4 to 5 hours | Serves 6

* 1 (16-ounce / 454-g) can low-sodium diced tomatoes
* 2 (15-ounce / 425-g) cans kidney or pinto beans, drained, divided
* 1 cup chopped onions
* 1 clove garlic, minced
* 1 (8¾-ounce / 248-g) can whole-kernel corn, drained
* ½ cup low-sodium picante sauce
* ½ cup water
* ½ teaspoon salt
* 1 teaspoon ground cumin
* 1 teaspoon dried oregano
* 1 green bell pepper, diced
* Reduced-fat shredded Cheddar cheese (optional)

1. Drain tomatoes, reserving juice. 2. Combine juice and 1 can beans in food processor bowl. Process until fairly smooth. 3. Combine all ingredients except green peppers and cheese in crock pot. 4. Cover. Cook on high 4 to 5 hours. 5. During last half hour add green peppers. 6. Ladle into bowls to serve. Top with cheese, if desired.

Mom's Chicken Noodle Goodness

Prep time: 15 minutes | Cook time: 4 to 8 hours | Serves 8 to 10

* 2 tablespoons olive oil
* 1 cup finely chopped onion
* 2 cups finely chopped celery
* 2 cups finely chopped carrot
* 2 small zucchini, finely chopped
* 1 teaspoon dried thyme
* 12 cups chicken broth
* 4 cups bite-size pieces cooked chicken
* 2 (10-ounce / 283-g) packages fresh baby spinach
* Salt and freshly ground black pepper
* 8 ounces (227 g) medium-width egg noodles, cooked al dente

1. Heat the oil in a large skillet over medium-high heat. Add the onion, celery, carrot, zucchini, and thyme and sauté until the vegetables are softened, about 7 minutes. 2. Transfer the contents of the skillet to the insert of a 5- to 7-quart crock pot. Stir in the broth, chicken, and spinach. 3. Cover and cook on high for 4 hours or on low for 8 hours. 4. Season with salt and pepper. Add the noodles to the soup, stir, cover, and let stand for 5 minutes before serving.

Curried Carrot Soup

Prep time: 20 minutes | Cook time: 2 hours | Serves 6 to 8

- 1 garlic clove, minced
- 1 large onion, chopped
- 2 tablespoons oil
- 1 tablespoon butter
- 1 teaspoon curry powder
- 1 tablespoon flour
- 4 cups chicken or vegetable broth
- 6 large carrots, sliced
- ¼ teaspoon salt
- ¼ teaspoon ground red pepper (optional)
- 1½ cups plain yogurt, or light sour cream

1. In skillet cook minced garlic and onion in oil and butter until limp but not brown. 2. Add curry and flour. Cook 30 seconds. Pour into crock pot. 3. Add chicken broth and carrots. 4. Cover. Cook on high for about 2 hours, or until carrots are soft. 5. Purée mixture in blender. Season with salt and pepper. Return to crock pot and keep warm until ready to serve. 6. Add a dollop of yogurt or sour cream to each serving.

Polish Sausage Stew

Prep time: 15 minutes | Cook time: 4 to 8 hours | Serves 6 to 8

- 1 (10¾-ounce / 305-g) can cream of celery soup
- ⅓ cup packed brown sugar
- 1 (27-ounce / 765-g) can sauerkraut, drained
- 1½ pounds (680 g) Polish sausage, cut into 2-inch pieces and browned
- 4 medium potatoes, cubed
- 1 cup chopped onions
- 1 cup shredded Monterey Jack cheese

1. Combine soup, sugar, and sauerkraut. Stir in sausage, potatoes, and onions. 2. Cover. Cook on low 8 hours, or on high 4 hours. 3. Stir in cheese and serve.

Chipotle Chicken Chili

Prep time: 20 minutes | Cook time: 7 to 8 hours | Serves 6

- 3 tablespoons extra-virgin olive oil, divided
- 1 pound (454 g) ground chicken
- ½ sweet onion, chopped
- 2 teaspoons minced garlic
- 1 (28-ounce / 794-g) can diced tomatoes
- 1 cup chicken broth
- 1 cup diced pumpkin
- 1 green bell pepper, diced
- 3 tablespoons chili powder
- 1 teaspoon chipotle chili powder
- 1 cup sour cream, for garnish
- 1 cup shredded Cheddar cheese, for garnish

1. Lightly grease the insert of the crock pot with 1 tablespoon of the olive oil. 2. In a large skillet over medium-high heat, heat the remaining 2 tablespoons of the olive oil. Add the chicken and sauté until it is cooked through, about 6 minutes. 3. Add the onion and garlic and sauté for an additional 3 minutes. 4. Transfer the chicken mixture to the insert and stir in the tomatoes, broth, pumpkin, bell pepper, chili powder, and chipotle chili powder. 5. Cover and cook on low for 7 to 8 hours. 6. Serve topped with the sour cream and cheese.

Mediterranean Vegetable Stew

Prep time: 25 minutes | Cook time: 8 to 10 hours | Serves 10

- 1 butternut squash, peeled, seeded, and cubed
- 2 cups unpeeled cubed eggplant
- 2 cups cubed zucchini
- 10 ounces (283 g) fresh okra, cut into slices
- 1 (8-ounce / 227-g) can tomato sauce
- 1 large yellow onion, chopped
- 1 ripe tomato, chopped
- 1 carrot, thinly sliced
- ½ cup vegetable stock
- ⅓ cup raisins
- 2 cloves garlic, minced
- ½ teaspoon ground cumin
- ½ teaspoon ground turmeric
- ¼ teaspoon red pepper flakes
- ¼ teaspoon ground cinnamon
- 1 teaspoon paprika

1. In the crock pot, combine the butternut squash, eggplant, zucchini, okra, tomato sauce, onion, tomato, carrot, vegetable stock, raisins, and garlic. Sprinkle in the cumin, turmeric, red pepper flakes, cinnamon, and paprika. 2. Cover and cook on low for 8 to 10 hours, or until the vegetables are fork-tender. Serve hot.

Wild Rice–Meatball Soup

Prep time: 15 minutes | Cook time: 8 hours | Serves 2

- ½ pound (227 g) frozen fully cooked meatballs
- 1 onion, chopped
- 2 large tomatoes, seeded and chopped
- 2 garlic cloves, minced
- ½ cup wild rice, rinsed
- 1 carrot, sliced
- 3 cups beef stock
- 1 bay leaf
- ½ teaspoon dried marjoram leaves
- ½ teaspoon salt
- ⅛ teaspoon freshly ground black pepper

1. In the crock pot, combine all the ingredients. 2. Cover and cook on low for 8 hours, or until the vegetables are tender. 3. Remove the bay leaf, ladle the soup into 2 bowls, and serve.

Taco Soup Plus

Prep time: 15 minutes | Cook time: 6 to 8 hours | Serves 6

- Soup:
- 1 pound (454 g) extra-lean ground beef or ground turkey
- 1 medium onion, chopped
- 1 medium green bell pepper, chopped
- 1 envelope dry reduced-sodium taco seasoning
- ½ cup water
- 4 cups reduced-sodium vegetable juice
- 1 cup chunky salsa
- Toppings:
- ¾ cup shredded lettuce
- 6 tablespoons fresh tomato, chopped
- 6 tablespoons reduced-fat Cheddar cheese, shredded
- ¼ cup green onions or chives, chopped
- ¼ cup fat-free sour cream or fat-free plain yogurt
- Baked tortilla or corn chips

1. Brown meat with onion in nonstick skillet. Drain. 2. Combine all soup ingredients in crock pot. 3. Cover. Cook on low 6 to 8 hours. 4. Serve with your choice of toppings.

Chili, Chicken, Corn Chowder

Prep time: 15 minutes | Cook time: 4 hours | Serves 6 to 8

- ¼ cup oil
- 1 large onion, diced
- 1 garlic clove, minced
- 1 rib celery, finely chopped
- 2 cups frozen or canned corn
- 2 cups cooked chicken,
- deboned and cubed
- 1 (4-ounce / 113-g) can diced green chilies
- ½ teaspoon black pepper
- 2 cups chicken broth
- Salt to taste
- 1 cup half-and-half

1. In saucepan, sauté onion, garlic, and celery in oil until limp. 2. Stir in corn, chicken, and chilies. Sauté for 2 to 3 minutes. 3. Combine all ingredients except half-and-half in crock pot. 4. Cover. Heat on low 4 hours. 5. Stir in half-and-half before serving. Do not boil, but be sure cream is heated through.

Busy Cook's Stew

Prep time: 30 minutes | Cook time: 6 to 8 hours | Serves 4 to 6

- 1 pound (454 g) boneless stew meat, cut up
- 1 (10¾-ounce / 305-g) can cream of mushroom soup
- 2 cups water
- 3 potatoes, cubed
- 3 carrots, diced
- 1 onion, chopped

1. Brown meat in large nonstick skillet. Don't crowd the skillet so the meat browns on all sides. (If your skillet is 10 inches or smaller, brown the beef in 2 batches.) 2. Place meat in crock pot. Add remaining ingredients in the order listed. Stir well after each addition. 3. Cover and cook on low 6 to 8 hours, or until meat and vegetables are tender but not mushy. Stir occasionally.

Miso Soup with Tofu, Shiitakes, and Shrimp

Prep time: 20 minutes | Cook time: 3 to 3½ hours | Serves 8

- 2 tablespoons vegetable oil
- 1 clove garlic, minced
- 1 teaspoon freshly grated ginger
- 8 ounces (227 g) shiitake mushrooms, stems removed, caps sliced
- ¼ cup light miso paste
- 6 cups vegetable or chicken broth
- 2 teaspoons soy sauce
- 1 pound (454 g) firm tofu, cut into ½-inch cubes
- 1 pound (454 g) medium shrimp, peeled and deveined, tails removed
- 6 green onions, finely chopped
- Toasted sesame oil for drizzling
- Toasted sesame seeds, for garnish

1. Heat the vegetable oil in a large skillet over high heat. Add the garlic and ginger and sauté until they are fragrant, about 1 minute. Add the mushrooms and toss with the garlic and ginger. 2. Transfer the contents of the skillet to the insert of a 5- to 7-quart crock pot. Stir in the miso, broth, and soy sauce. 3. Cover and cook on high for 2½ to 3 hours. Add the tofu and shrimp, cover, turn the cooker to low, and cook until the shrimp are pink and cooked through, about 30 minutes. 4. Add the green onions to the soup and serve drizzled with the sesame oil and garnished with sesame seeds.

Cheeseburger Soup

Prep time: 15 minutes | Cook time: 8 to 9 hours | Serves 6

- 1 pound (454 g) ground turkey
- 1 cup chopped onions
- ½ cup chopped green bell peppers
- 2 ribs celery, chopped
- 1 (20-ounce / 567-g) beef
- broth
- 1 cup non-fat milk
- 2 cups water
- 2 tablespoons flour
- 8 ounces (227 g) low-fat Cheddar cheese, shredded

1. Brown turkey in nonstick skillet. Spoon into crock pot. 2. Add vegetables to crock pot. 3. Heat broth, milk, and water in skillet. Sprinkle flour over liquid. Stir until smooth and let boil for 3 minutes. 4. Pour into crock pot. 5. Cover. Cook on low 6 hours. Then add cheese and cook another 2 to 3 hours.

Lidia's Egg Drop Soup

Prep time: 10 minutes | Cook time: 1 hour | Serves 8

- 2 (14½-ounce / 411-g) cans fat-free, low-sodium chicken broth
- 1 quart water
- 2 tablespoons fish sauce
- ¼ teaspoon salt
- 4 tablespoons cornstarch
- 1 cup cold water
- 2 eggs, beaten
- 1 chopped green onion
- ¼ teaspoon black pepper

1. Combine broth and water in large saucepan. 2. Add fish sauce and salt. Bring to boil. 3. Mix cornstarch into cold water until smooth. Add to soup. Bring to boil while stirring. Remove from heat. 4. Pour beaten eggs into thickened broth, but do not stir. Instead, pull fork through soup with 2 strokes. 5. Transfer to crock pot. Add green onions and pepper. 6. Cover. Cook on low 1 hour. Keep warm in cooker or serve.

Chinese Chicken Soup

Prep time: 5 minutes | Cook time: 1 to 2 hours | Serves 6

- 3 (14½-ounce / 411-g) cans chicken broth
- 1 (16-ounce / 454-g) package frozen stir-fry vegetable blend
- 2 cups cooked chicken, cubed
- 1 teaspoon minced fresh ginger root
- 1 teaspoon soy sauce

1. Mix all ingredients in crock pot. 2. Cover and cook on high for 1 to 2 hours, depending upon how crunchy or soft you like your vegetables to be.

Many-Veggies Beef Stew

Prep time: 25 minutes | Cook time: 10 to 11 hours | Serves 14 to 18

- 2 to 3 pounds (907 g to 1.4 kg) beef, cubed
- 1 (16-ounce / 454-g) package frozen green beans or mixed vegetables
- 1 (16-ounce / 454-g) package frozen corn
- 1 (16-ounce / 454-g) package frozen peas
- 2 pounds (907 g) carrots, chopped
- 1 large onion, chopped
- 4 medium potatoes, peeled and chopped
- 1 (10¾-ounce / 305-g) can tomato soup
- 1 (10¾-ounce / 305-g) can celery soup
- 1 (10¾-ounce / 305-g) can mushroom soup
- Bell pepper, chopped (optional)

1. Combine all ingredients in 2 (4-quart) crock pots (this is a very large recipe). 2. Cover. Cook on low 10 to 11 hours.

Split Pea Soup

Prep time: 10 minutes | Cook time: 8 to 10 hours | Serves 2

- 1 cup dried green split peas, rinsed
- ¼ cup diced ham
- ¼ cup diced carrots
- ¼ cup diced onion
- ¼ cup diced celery
- 1 garlic clove, minced
- 3 cups low-sodium chicken broth
- 1 sprig fresh thyme
- ⅛ teaspoon sea salt

1. Put all the ingredients to the crock pot and stir to combine. 2. Cover and cook on low for 8 to 10 hours. Remove the thyme sprig before serving.

Chicken Rice and Veggies Soup

Prep time: 30 minutes | Cook time: 4 to 8 hours | Serves 8

- 4 cups chicken broth
- 4 cups cooked chicken, cubed or shredded
- 1⅓ cups cut-up celery
- 1⅓ cups diced carrots
- 1 quart water
- 1 cup long-grain rice, uncooked

1. Put all ingredients in crock pot. 2. Cover and cook on low 4 to 8 hours, or until vegetables are cooked to your liking.

Onion Soup

Prep time: 30 minutes | Cook time: 6 to 8 hours | Serves 8

- 3 medium onions, thinly sliced
- 2 tablespoons butter
- 2 tablespoons vegetable oil
- 1 teaspoon salt
- 1 tablespoon sugar
- 2 tablespoons flour
- 1 quart fat-free, low-sodium vegetable broth
- ½ cup dry white wine
- Slices of French bread
- ½ cup grated fat-free Swiss or Parmesan cheese

1. Sauté onions in butter and oil in covered skillet until soft. Uncover. Add salt and sugar. Cook 15 minutes. Stir in flour. Cook 3 more minutes. 2. Combine onions, broth, and wine in crock pot. 3. Cover. Cook on low 6 to 8 hours. 4. Toast bread. Sprinkle with grated cheese and then broil. 5. Dish soup into individual bowls; then float a slice of broiled bread on top of each serving of soup.

Barley-Mushroom Soup

Prep time: 15 minutes | Cook time: 7 to 8 hours | Serves 8

- 6 cups sliced fresh mushrooms
- 2 large onions, chopped
- 3 cloves garlic, minced
- 1 cup chopped celery
- 1 cup chopped carrots
- 5 cups water, divided
- ¼ cup dry quick-cooking pearl barley
- 4 cups low-sodium beef broth
- 4 teaspoons Worcestershire
- sauce
- 1 to 1½ teaspoons salt (optional)
- 1½ teaspoons dried basil
- 1½ teaspoons dried parsley flakes
- 1 teaspoon dill weed
- 1½ teaspoons dried oregano
- ½ teaspoon salt-free seasoning blend
- ½ teaspoon dried thyme
- ½ teaspoon garlic powder

1. Combine all ingredients in crock pot. 2. Cook on low 7 to 8 hours, or until vegetables are done to your liking.

Creamy Corn and Turkey Soup

Prep time: 15 minutes | Cook time: 3 to 8 hours | Serves 5 to 6

- 2 cups cooked turkey, shredded
- 1 cup milk
- 2 cups chicken broth
- 1 (15-ounce / 425-g) can
- Mexican-style corn
- 4 ounces (113 g) cream cheese, cubed
- 1 red bell pepper, chopped (optional)

1. Place all ingredients in crock pot. 2. Cover and cook on low 7 to 8 hours, or on high 3 hours.

Wonderful Clam Chowder

Prep time: 15 minutes | Cook time: 6 to 7 hours | Serves 4 to 6

- 2 (12-ounce / 340-g) cans evaporated milk
- 1 evaporated milk can of water
- 2 (6-ounce / 170-g) cans whole clams, undrained
- 1 (6-ounce / 170-g) can minced clams, undrained
- 1 small onion, chopped
- 2 small potatoes, diced
- 2 tablespoons cornstarch
- ¼ cup water

1. Combine all ingredients except cornstarch and ¼ cup water in crock pot. 2. Cover. Cook on low 6 to 7 hours. 3. One hour before end of cooking time, mix cornstarch and ¼ cup water together. When smooth, stir into soup. Stir until soup thickens.

Bean Soup

Prep time: 10 minutes | Cook time: 5½ to 13 hours | Serves 10 to 12

- 1 cup dry Great Northern beans
- 1 cup dry red beans or pinto beans
- 4 cups water
- 1 (28-ounce / 794-g) can diced tomatoes
- 1 medium onion, chopped
- 2 tablespoons vegetable
- bouillon granules, or 4 bouillon cubes
- 2 garlic cloves, minced
- 2 teaspoons Italian seasoning, crushed
- 1 (9-ounce / 255-g) package frozen green beans, thawed

1. Soak and rinse dried beans. 2. Combine all ingredients except green beans in crock pot. 3. Cover. Cook on high 5½ to 6½ hours, or on low 11 to 13 hours. 4. Stir green beans into soup during last 2 hours.

Curried Meatball Soup

Prep time: 40 minutes | Cook time: 4 hours | Serves 8

- Meat Balls:
- 1 cup cooked long-grain rice
- 1½ pounds (680 g) 85-percent lean ground beef
- 1 teaspoon sweet curry powder
- 2 tablespoons soy sauce
- 4 green onions, finely chopped, using the white and tender green parts
- 1 tablespoon Major Grey's chutney or other mild
- chutney
- 1 large egg, beaten
- Soup:
- 7 cups beef broth
- ½ cup soy sauce
- 1 bunch bok choy, cut into 1-inch pieces (about 2 cups)
- 1 cup snow peas, ends trimmed and strings removed
- 2 cups fresh bean sprouts or other sprouts such as radish or broccoli, for garnish

1. Put all the meatball ingredients in a large bowl and stir to combine. Using a small scoop, form the meat into 1-inch balls. 2. Add the broth and soy sauce to the insert of a 5- to 7-quart crock pot. 3. Add the meatballs, cover, and cook on high for 3 hours, until the meatballs float to the top. Skim off any foam that may have formed from the top of the broth. 4. Add the bok choy and snow peas to the cooker and cook on low for an additional 1 hour, until the bok choy is tender. 5. Serve the soup garnished with the fresh bean sprouts.

Green Chili Corn Chowder

Prep time: 15 minutes | Cook time: 7¼ to 8¼ hours | Serves 8

- 1 (16-ounce / 454-g) can cream-style corn
- 3 potatoes, peeled and diced
- 2 tablespoons chopped fresh chives
- 1 (4-ounce / 113-g) can diced green chilies, drained
- 1 (2-ounce / 57-g) jar chopped pimentos, drained
- ½ to ¾ cup chopped cooked ham
- 2 (10½-ounce / 298-g) cans chicken broth
- Salt to taste
- Pepper to taste
- Tabasco sauce to taste
- 1 cup milk
- Shredded Monterey Jack cheese

1. Combine all ingredients except milk and cheese in crock pot. 2. Cover. Cook on low 7 to 8 hours or until potatoes are tender. 3. Stir in milk. Heat until hot. 4. Top individual servings with cheese. Serve.

Taco Chicken Soup

Prep time: 10 minutes | Cook time: 5 to 7 hours | Serves 4 to 6

- 1 envelope dry reduced-sodium taco seasoning
- 1 (32-ounce / 907-g) can low-sodium V-8 juice
- 1 (16-ounce / 454-g) jar salsa
- 1 (15-ounce / 425-g) can black beans
- 1 cup frozen corn
- 1 cup frozen peas
- 2 whole chicken breasts, cooked and shredded

1. Combine all ingredients except corn, peas, and chicken in crock pot. 2. Cover. Cook on low 4 to 6 hours. Add remaining vegetables and chicken 1 hour before serving.

German Potato Soup

Prep time: 15 minutes | Cook time: 4 to 10 hours | Serves 6 to 8

- 1 onion, chopped
- 1 leek, trimmed and diced
- 2 carrots, diced
- 1 cup chopped cabbage
- ¼ cup chopped fresh parsley
- 4 cups beef broth
- 1 pound (454 g) potatoes, diced
- 1 bay leaf
- 1 to 2 teaspoons black pepper
- 1 teaspoon salt (optional)
- ½ teaspoon caraway seeds (optional)
- ¼ teaspoon nutmeg
- 1 pound (454 g) bacon, cooked and crumbled
- ½ cup sour cream

1. Combine all ingredients except bacon and sour cream. 2. Cover. Cook on low 8 to 10 hours, or on high 4 to 5 hours. 3. Remove bay leaf. Use a slotted spoon to remove potatoes. Mash potatoes and mix with sour cream. Return to crock pot. Stir in. Add bacon and mix together thoroughly.

Cumin and Cauliflower Soup

Prep time: 12 minutes | Cook time: 2 to 4 hours | Serves 6

- 2 tablespoons rapeseed oil
- 1 bay leaf
- 2 teaspoons cumin seeds
- 5 garlic cloves, sliced
- 2 fresh green chiles
- 1 head of cauliflower, chopped
- 1 teaspoon sea salt
- 4 cups hot water

1. Preheat the crock pot on high. 2. Heat the oil in a frying pan (or in the crock pot if you have a sear setting) and add the bay leaf and the cumin seeds. When they are aromatic, stir in the garlic and sauté until it just browns. Pour the whole thing into the crock pot. 3. Roughly chop the chiles and add them to the crock pot, along with the chopped cauliflower, salt, and water. 4. Cover and cook on low for 4 hours, or on high for 2 hours. 5. Remove the bay leaf. Using an immersion or regular blender, purée the soup until it's smooth. Check the seasonings and adjust if required. 6. To garnish, dry-fry a few cumin seeds until fragrant, about 1 minute. Serve in small bowls and top with a sprinkling of roasted cumin.

Chicken and Shrimp Bouillabaisse

Prep time: 20 minutes | Cook time: 7⅓ hours | Serves 2

- 4 boneless, skinless chicken thighs, cut into strips
- 1 onion, chopped
- 3 garlic cloves, minced
- 1 cup sliced fennel
- 2 large tomatoes, seeded and chopped
- 2 Yukon Gold potatoes, cubed
- 2 cups clam juice
- ½ cup dry white wine
- 1 teaspoon dried thyme leaves
- ½ teaspoon salt
- ⅛ teaspoon freshly ground black pepper
- 1 pinch saffron
- ½ pound (227 g) medium shrimp, peeled and deveined
- 1 teaspoon minced fresh rosemary leaves

1. In the crock pot, combine all the ingredients except the shrimp and rosemary, and mix well. 2. Cover and cook on low for 7 hours. 3. Add the shrimp and rosemary. Cover and cook on high for 20 minutes, or until the shrimp curl and turn pink. 4. Ladle the stew into 2 bowls and serve.

Potato Chowder

Prep time: 15 minutes | Cook time: 8½ to 10½ hours | Serves 12

- 8 cups peeled, diced potatoes
- 3 (14½-ounce / 411-g) cans chicken broth
- 1 (10¾-ounce / 305-g) can cream of chicken soup
- ¼ teaspoon pepper
- 1 (8-ounce / 227-g) package cream cheese, cubed

1. In crock pot, combine potatoes, chicken broth, chicken soup, and pepper. 2. Cover and cook on low 8 to 10 hours, or until potatoes are tender. 3. Add cream cheese, stirring until well blended. 4. Heat until cheese melts and soup is hot throughout.

Split Pea Soup with Ham

Prep time: 15 minutes | Cook time: 4 hours | Serves 8

- 2½ quarts water
- 1 ham hock or pieces of cut-up ham
- 2½ cups split peas, dried
- 1 medium onion, chopped
- 3 medium carrots, cut in small pieces
- Salt and pepper to taste

1. Bring water to a boil in a saucepan on your stovetop. 2. Place all other ingredients into crock pot. Add water and stir together well. 3. Cover and cook on high for 4 hours, or until vegetables are tender. 4. If you've cooked a ham hock, remove it from the soup and debone the meat. Stir cut-up chunks of meat back into the soup before serving.

Vegetable Beef Soup

Prep time: 15 minutes | Cook time: 4 to 6 hours | Serves 8

- 1 pound (454 g) extra-lean ground beef
- 1 (14½-ounce / 411-g) can low-sodium, stewed tomatoes
- 1 (10¾-ounce / 305-g) can low-sodium tomato soup
- 1 onion, chopped
- 2 cups water
- 1 (15½-ounce / 439-g) can garbanzo beans, drained
- 1 (15¼-ounce / 432-g) can corn, drained
- 1 (14½-ounce / 411-g) can sliced carrots, drained
- 1 cup diced potatoes
- 1 cup chopped celery
- ½ teaspoon salt
- ¼ teaspoon black pepper
- Chopped garlic to taste (optional)

1. Sauté ground beef in nonstick skillet. 2. Combine all ingredients in crock pot. 3. Cook on low 4 to 6 hours.

Chapter ⑦

Snacks and Appetizers

Butterscotch Haystacks

Prep time: 15 minutes | Cook time: 15 minutes | Makes 3 dozen pieces

- 2 (6-ounce / 170-g) packages butterscotch chips
- ¾ cup chopped almonds
- 1 (5-ounce / 142-g) can chow mein noodles

1. Turn cooker to high. Place chips in crock pot. Stir every few minutes until they're melted. 2. When the chips are completely melted, gently stir in almonds and noodles. 3. When well mixed, drop by teaspoonfuls onto waxed paper. 4. Let stand until haystacks are set, or speed things up by placing them in the fridge until set. 5. Serve, or store in a covered container, placing waxed paper between layers of candy. Keep in a cool, dry place.

Mustard-Lovers' Party Dogs

Prep time: 15 minutes | Cook time: 1 to 2 hours | Serves 12

- 12 hot dogs, cut into bite-size pieces
- 1 cup grape jelly
- 1 cup prepared mustard

1. Place all ingredients in crock pot. Stir well. 2. Turn on high until mixture boils. Stir. 3. Turn to low and bring to the buffet table.

Orange Chipotle Wings

Prep time: 15 minutes | Cook time: 3 hours | Serves 8

- 3 pounds (1.4 kg) chicken wing drumettes
- 1 medium red onion, finely chopped
- 6 chipotle chiles in adobo, finely chopped
- 1 teaspoon ground cumin
- 2 cloves garlic, minced
- 1½ cups orange juice
- ½ cup honey
- ½ cup ketchup
- ½ cup finely chopped fresh cilantro

1. Coat the insert of a 5- to 7-quart crock pot with nonstick cooking spray. 2. Arrange the wings on a rack in a baking sheet and broil until the wings are crispy on one side. 3. Turn the wings and broil until crispy and browned, another 5 minutes. 4. Remove the wings from the oven. If you would like to do this step ahead of time, cool the wings and refrigerate for up to 2 days; other wise, place the wings in the prepared slow-cooker insert. 5. Combine the remaining ingredients in a mixing bowl, pour over the wings, and turn the wings to coat with the sauce. 6. Cover and cook the wings on high for 3 hours, until they are cooked through; turn them twice during the cooking process to ensure even cooking. 7. Serve the wings from the cooker set on warm.

Slim Dunk

Prep time: 10 minutes | Cook time: 1 hour | Serves 12

- 2 cups fat-free sour cream
- ¼ cup fat-free miracle whip salad dressing
- 1 (10-ounce / 283-g) package frozen chopped spinach, squeezed dry and chopped
- 1 (1.8-ounce / 51-g) envelope dry leek soup mix
- ¼ cup red bell pepper, minced

1. Combine all ingredients in crock pot. Mix well. 2. Cover. Cook on high 1 hour. 3. Serve.

Curried Almonds

Prep time: 5 minutes | Cook time: 3 to 4½ hours | Makes 4 cups nuts

- 2 tablespoons butter, melted
- 1 tablespoon curry powder
- ½ teaspoon seasoned salt
- 1 pound (454 g) blanched almonds

1. Combine butter with curry powder and seasoned salt. 2. Pour over almonds in crock pot. Mix to coat well. 3. Cover. Cook on low 2 to 3 hours. Turn to high. Uncover cooker and cook 1 to 1½ hours. 4. Serve hot or cold.

Warm Clam Dip

Prep time: 15 minutes | Cook time: 2 to 3 hours | Serves 6 to 8

- 2 (8-ounce / 227-g) packages cream cheese at room temperature and cut into cubes
- ½ cup mayonnaise
- 3 green onions, finely chopped, using the white and tender green parts
- 2 cloves garlic, minced
- 3 (8-ounce / 227-g) cans minced or chopped clams, drained with ¼ cup clam juice reserved
- 1 tablespoon Worcestershire sauce
- 2 teaspoons anchovy paste
- ¼ cup finely chopped fresh Italian parsley

1. Coat the insert of a 1½- to 3-quart crock pot with nonstick cooking spray. Combine all the ingredients in a large mixing bowl, adding the clam juice to thin the dip. 2. Transfer the mixture to the crock pot, cover, and cook on low for 2 to 3 hours, until bubbling. 3. Serve from the cooker set on warm.

Barbecued Lil' Smokies

Prep time: 5 minutes | Cook time: 4 hours | Serves 48 to 60 as an appetizer

- 4 (16-ounce / 454-g) packages little smokies
- 1 (18-ounce / 510-g) bottle barbecue sauce

1. Mix ingredients together in crock pot. 2. Cover and cook on low for 4 hours.

Refried Bean Dip

Prep time: 20 minutes | Cook time: 2 to 3 hours | Serves 8

- 8 ounces (227 g) spicy sausages, such as chorizo, andouille, or Italian, removed from its casing
- 1 medium onion, chopped
- 2 Anaheim chiles, seeded and chopped
- 1 medium red or yellow bell pepper, seeded and chopped
- 2 (14- to 15-ounce / 397- to 425-g) cans refried beans (nonfat are fine here)
- 2 cups finely shredded mild Cheddar cheese, or 1 cup each finely shredded Monterey Jack and sharp Cheddar cheese
- 2 tablespoons finely chopped fresh cilantro
- Tortilla chips for serving

1. Spray the insert of a 1½ - to 3-quart crock pot with nonstick cooking spray. Cook the sausage in a medium skillet over high heat until it is no longer pink, breaking up any large pieces with the side of a spoon. Drain the sausage and put it in a mixing bowl to cool. Add the onion, chiles, and bell pepper to the same skillet and sauté until the bell pepper is softened, about 5 minutes. Add to the bowl with the sausage and allow to cool slightly. Add the refried beans to the bowl and stir to blend. 2. Spoon half the bean mixture into the slow-cooker insert and sprinkle with half the cheese. Top with the remaining beans and cheese and sprinkle with the cilantro. Cover and cook on low for 2 to 3 hours. 3. Serve from the cooker set at warm and accompany with sturdy tortilla chips.

Chili Nuts

Prep time: 5 minutes | Cook time: 2 to 2½ hours | Makes 5 cups nuts

- ¼ cup butter, melted
- 2 (12-ounce / 340-g) cans cocktail peanuts
- 1 (1.6-ounce / 45-g) package chili seasoning mix

1. Pour butter over nuts in crock pot. 2. Sprinkle in dry chili mix. Toss together. Cover. Heat on low 2 to 2½ hours. Turn to

high. Remove lid and cook 10 to 15 minutes. 3. Serve warm or cool.

The Best Artichoke Spinach Dip on the Planet

Prep time: 15 minutes | Cook time: 2 to 3 hours | Serves 8

- 6 strips bacon, cut into ½-inch pieces
- 1 medium onion, finely chopped
- 1 (16-ounce / 454-g) package frozen chopped spinach, defrosted and drained thoroughly
- 1 (16-ounce / 454-g) package frozen artichoke hearts, defrosted, drained,
- and coarsely chopped, or 2 (14- to 15-ounce / 397- to 425-g) cans artichoke hearts, drained and coarsely chopped
- ¼ teaspoon freshly ground black pepper
- 1½ cups mayonnaise
- 2 cups shredded sharp white Cheddar cheese

1. Cook the bacon in a large skillet until crisp and remove it to paper towels to drain. Remove all but 2 tablespoons of the bacon drippings from the pan and heat over medium-high heat. 2. Add the onion and sauté until it begins to sof ten, about 2 minutes. Add the spinach and artichoke hearts and sauté until the water in the pan has evaporated. Season the mixture with the pepper and turn it out into the insert of a 1½- to 3-quart crock pot. Add the mayonnaise and cheese to the cooker and stir until blended. Cover and cook on low for 2 to 3 hours. 3. Garnish the dip with the bacon bits and serve from the cooker set on warm.

Crock Pot Candy

Prep time: 10 minutes | Cook time: 2 hours | Makes 80 to 100 pieces

- 1½ pounds (680 g) almond bark, broken
- 1 (4-ounce / 113-g) Baker's Brand German sweet chocolate bar, broken
- 8 ounces (227 g) chocolate
- chips
- 8 ounces (227 g) peanut butter chips
- 2 pounds (907 g) lightly salted or unsalted peanuts

1. Spray inside of cooker with nonstick cooking spray. 2. Layer ingredients into crock pot in the order given above. 3. Cook on low 2 hours. Do not stir or lift the lid during the cooking time. 4. After 2 hours, mix well. 5. Drop by teaspoonfuls onto waxed paper. Refrigerate for approximately 45 minutes before serving or storing.

Tangy Meatballs

Prep time: 15 minutes | Cook time: 2 to 4 hours | Makes 50 to 60 meatballs

- 2 pounds (907 g) precooked meatballs
- 1 (16-ounce / 454-g) bottle barbecue sauce
- 8 ounces (227 g) grape jelly

1. Place meatballs in crock pot. 2. Combine barbecue sauce and jelly in medium-sized mixing bowl. 3. Pour over meatballs and stir well. 4. Cover and cook on high 2 hours, or on low 4 hours. 5. Turn to low and serve.

Garlic Swiss Fondue

Prep time: 10 minutes | Cook time: 2 hours | Makes 3 cups

- 4 cups shredded Swiss cheese
- 1 (10¾-ounce / 305-g) can condensed cheddar cheese soup, undiluted
- 2 tablespoons sherry or chicken broth
- 1 tablespoon Dijon mustard
- 2 garlic cloves, minced
- 2 teaspoons hot pepper sauce
- Cubed French bread baguette
- Sliced apples
- Seedless red grapes

1. In a 1½-quart crock pot, mix the first six ingredients. Cook, covered, on low 2 to 2½ hours or until the cheese is melted, stirring every 30 minutes. Serve warm with bread cubes and fruit.

Mornay Dip for Crab Claws and Shrimp

Prep time: 10 minutes | Cook time: 2 to 3 hours | Serves 8

- 2 tablespoons unsalted butter
- 2 medium shallots, finely chopped
- 2 teaspoons Old Bay seasoning
- 2 tablespoons all-purpose flour
- 2 cups lobster stock
- ¼ cup cream sherry
- 1 cup heavy cream
- ¼ cup finely chopped fresh Italian parsley

1. Melt the butter in a small saucepan over medium-high heat. Add the shallots and seasoning and cook for 2 minutes, until the shallots are softened. Add the flour and cook for 3 minutes, whisking constantly. Gradually whisk in the stock and sherry and bring the mixture to a boil. 2. Stir in the cream and parsley to combine. Transfer to the insert of a 1½- to 3-quart crock

pot. Cover and cook on low for 2 to 3 hours. 3. Serve from the cooker set on warm.

Meaty Buffet Favorites

Prep time: 5 minutes | Cook time: 2 hours | Serves 24

- 1 cup tomato sauce
- 1 teaspoon Worcestershire sauce
- ½ teaspoon prepared mustard
- 2 tablespoons brown sugar
- 1 pound (454 g) prepared meatballs or mini-wieners

1. Mix first four ingredients in crock pot. 2. Add meatballs or mini-wieners. 3. Cover and cook on high for 2 hours. Turn to low and serve as an appetizer from the crock pot.

Snack Mix

Prep time: 10 minutes | Cook time: 2 hours | Serves 10 to 14

- 8 cups Chex cereal, of any combination
- 6 cups pretzels
- 6 tablespoons butter, melted
- 2 tablespoons Worcestershire sauce
- 1 teaspoon seasoned salt
- ½ teaspoon garlic powder
- ½ teaspoon onion salt
- ½ teaspoon onion powder

1. Combine first two ingredients in crock pot. 2. Combine butter and seasonings. Pour over dry mixture. Toss until well mixed. 3. Cover. Cook on low 2 hours, stirring every 30 minutes.

Cheesy Tomato Pizza Fondue

Prep time: 15 minutes | Cook time: 1 hour | Serves 4 to 6

- 1 (1-pound / 454-g) block of cheese, your choice of good melting cheese, cut in ½-inch cubes
- 2 cups shredded Mozzarella cheese
- 1 (19-ounce / 539-g) can Italian-style stewed tomatoes with juice
- Loaf of Italian bread, slices toasted and then cut into 1-inch cubes

1. Place cheese cubes, shredded Mozzarella cheese, and tomatoes in a lightly greased crock pot. 2. Cover and cook on high 45 to 60 minutes, or until cheese is melted. 3. Stir occasionally and scrape down sides of crock pot with rubber spatula to prevent scorching. 4. Reduce heat to low and serve. (Fondue will keep a smooth consistency for up to 4 hours.) 5. Serve with toasted bread cubes for dipping.

Spicy Rasta Wings

Prep time: 15 minutes | Cook time: 3 hours | Serves 8

- 3 pounds (1.4 kg) chicken wing drumettes
- 2 teaspoons jerk seasoning
- 1½ cups mango nectar
- ¼ cup firmly packed light brown sugar

1. Coat the insert of a 5- to 7-quart crock pot with nonstick cooking spray. 2. Arrange the wings on a rack in a baking sheet and broil until the wings are crispy on one side. 3. Turn the wings and broil until crispy and browned, another 5 minutes. 4. Remove the wings from the oven. If you would like to do this step ahead of time, cool the wings and refrigerate for up to 2 days; other wise, place the wings in the prepared slow-cooker insert. 5. Combine the remaining ingredients in a mixing bowl, pour over the wings, and turn the wings to coat with the sauce. 6. Cover and cook on high for 3 hours, turning the wings twice during the cooking time. 7. Serve the wings from the cooker set on warm.

Crispy Snack Mix

Prep time: 10 minutes | Cook time: 2½ hours | Makes about 2½ quarts

- 4½ cups crispy chow mein noodles
- 4 cups Rice Chex
- 1 (9¾-ounce / 276-g) can salted cashews
- 1 cup flaked coconut,
- toasted
- ½ cup butter, melted
- 2 tablespoons reduced-sodium soy sauce
- 2¼ teaspoons curry powder
- ¾ teaspoon ground ginger

1. In a 5-quart crock pot, combine the noodles, cereal, cashews and coconut. In a small bowl, whisk the butter, soy sauce, curry powder and ginger; drizzle over cereal mixture and mix well. 2. Cover and cook on low for 2½ hours, stirring every 30 minutes. Serve warm or at room temperature.

Creamy Artichoke Dip

Prep time: 20 minutes | Cook time: 1 hour | Makes 5 cups

- 2 (14-ounce / 397-g) cans water-packed artichoke hearts, rinsed, drained and coarsely chopped
- 2 cups shredded part-skim mozzarella cheese
- 1 (8-ounce / 227-g) package cream cheese,
- cubed
- 1 cup shredded Parmesan cheese
- ½ cup mayonnaise
- ½ cup shredded Swiss cheese
- 2 tablespoons lemon juice
- 2 tablespoons plain yogurt

- 1 tablespoon seasoned salt
- 1 tablespoon chopped seeded jalapeno pepper
- 1 teaspoon garlic powder
- Tortilla chips

1. In a 3-quart crock pot, combine the first 11 ingredients. Cover and cook on low for 1 hour or until heated through. Serve with tortilla chips.

Sweet 'n Sour Meatballs

Prep time: 10 minutes | Cook time: 2 to 4 hours | Serves 15 to 20

- 1 (12-ounce / 340-g) jar grape jelly
- 1 (12-ounce / 340-g) jar chili sauce
- 2 (1-pound / 454-g) bags prepared frozen meatballs, thawed

1. Combine jelly and sauce in crock pot. Stir well. 2. Add meatballs. Stir to coat. 3. Cover and heat on low 4 hours, or on high 2 hours. Keep crock pot on low while serving.

Liver Paté

Prep time: 15 minutes | Cook time: 4 to 5 hours | Makes 1½ cups paté

- 1 pound (454 g) chicken livers
- ½ cup dry wine
- 1 teaspoon instant chicken bouillon
- 1 teaspoon minced parsley
- 1 tablespoon instant minced
- onion
- ¼ teaspoon ground ginger
- ½ teaspoon seasoned salt
- 1 tablespoon soy sauce
- ¼ teaspoon dry mustard
- ¼ cup soft butter
- 1 tablespoon brandy

1. In crock pot, combine all ingredients except butter and brandy. 2. Cover. Cook on low 4 to 5 hours. Let stand in liquid until cool. 3. Drain. Place in blender or food grinder. Add butter and brandy. Process until smooth. 4. Serve.

Slow Cooked Smokies

Prep time: 5 minutes | Cook time: 6 to 7 hours | Serves 12 to 16

- 2 pounds (907 g) miniature smoked sausage links
- 1 (28-ounce / 794-g) bottle barbecue sauce
- 1¼ cups water
- 3 tablespoons Worcestershire sauce
- 3 tablespoons steak sauce
- ½ teaspoon pepper

1. In a crock pot, combine all ingredients. Mix well. 2. Cover and cook on low 6 to 7 hours.

Kielbasa in Spicy Barbecue Sauce

Prep time: 20 minutes | Cook time: 4 to 5 hours | Serves 8

- 2 cups ketchup
- ½ cup firmly packed light brown sugar
- 1 tablespoon Worcestershire sauce
- 1 teaspoon Creole mustard
- 1 teaspoon hot sauce
- 1 medium onion, finely chopped
- ½ cup bourbon
- 2 pounds (907 g) kielbasa or other smoked sausages, cut into ½-inch rounds

1. Combine all the ingredients in the insert of a 3- to 5-quart crock pot. Cover and cook on low for 4 to 5 hours, until the sausage is heated through. 2. Serve the kielbasa from the cooker set on warm, with 6-inch skewers.

Sausages in Wine

Prep time: 15 minutes | Cook time: 1 hour | Serves 6

- 1 cup dry red wine
- 2 tablespoons currant jelly
- 6 to 8 mild Italian sausages or Polish sausages

1. Place wine and jelly in crock pot. Heat until jelly is dissolved and sauce begins to simmer. Add sausages. 2. Cover and cook on high 45 minutes to 1 hour, or until sausages are cooked through and lightly glazed. 3. Transfer sausages to a cutting board and slice. Serve.

Maytag Blue and Walnut Dip with Apple Dippers

Prep time: 10 minutes | Cook time: 2 to 3 hours | Serves 8

- 2 (8-ounce / 227-g) packages cream cheese at room temperature
- ½ cup mayonnaise
- 2 tablespoons Ruby Port
- 6 drops Tabasco sauce
- 1 cup chopped walnuts
- 2 cups crumbled Maytag blue cheese
- 4 to 6 Granny Smith Apples, cored and cut into 8 wedges each, for serving
- Crackers for serving

1. Coat the insert of a 1½- to 3-quart crock pot with nonstick cooking spray. Put the cream cheese, mayonnaise, port, Tabasco, walnuts, and blue cheese in a mixing bowl and stir until blended. 2. Transfer the mixture to the slow-cooker insert. Cover and cook on low for 2 to 3 hours, until heated through

and bubbly. 3. Serve from the cooker set on warm with the apple wedges and crackers.

Jalapeno Spinach Dip

Prep time: 10 minutes | Cook time: 2 hours | Serves 6

- 2 (10-ounce / 283-g) packages frozen chopped spinach, thawed and squeezed dry
- 2 (8-ounce / 227-g) packages cream cheese, softened
- 1 cup grated Parmesan cheese
- 1 cup half-and-half cream
- ½ cup finely chopped onion
- ¼ cup chopped seeded jalapeno peppers
- 2 teaspoons Worcestershire sauce
- 2 teaspoons hot pepper sauce
- 1 teaspoon garlic powder
- 1 teaspoon dill weed
- Tortilla chips

1. In a small bowl, combine the cream cheese, dressing, sour cream and blue cheese. Transfer to a 3-quart crock pot. Layer with chicken, wing sauce and 1 cup cheese. Cover and cook on low for 2 to 3 hours or until heated through. 2. Sprinkle with remaining cheese and onion. Serve with tortilla chips.

"Baked" Brie with Cranberry Chutney

Prep time: 10 minutes | Cook time: 4 hours | Serves 8 to 10

- 1 cup fresh or dried cranberries
- ½ cup brown sugar
- ⅓ cup cider vinegar
- 2 tablespoons water or orange juice
- 2 teaspoons minced crystallized ginger
- ¼ teaspoon cinnamon
- ⅛ teaspoon ground cloves
- Oil
- 1 (8-ounce / 227-g) round of Brie cheese
- 1 tablespoon sliced almonds, toasted
- Crackers

1. Mix together cranberries, brown sugar, vinegar, water or juice, ginger, cinnamon, and cloves in crock pot. 2. Cover. Cook on low 4 hours. Stir once near the end to see if it is thickening. If not, remove lid, turn heat to high and cook 30 minutes without lid. 3. Put cranberry chutney in covered container and chill for up to 2 weeks. When ready to serve, bring to room temperature. 4. Brush ovenproof plate with oil, place unpeeled Brie on plate, and bake uncovered at 350ºF (180ºC) for 9 minutes, until cheese is soft and partially melted. Remove from oven. 5. Top with at least half the chutney and garnish with almonds. Serve with crackers.

Buffalo Wing Dip

Prep time: 20 minutes | Cook time: 2 hours | Makes 6 cups

- 2 (8-ounce / 227-g) packages cream cheese, softened
- ½ cup ranch salad dressing
- ½ cup sour cream
- 5 tablespoons crumbled blue cheese
- 2 cups shredded cooked chicken
- ½ cup Buffalo wing sauce
- 2 cups shredded cheddar cheese, divided
- 1 green onion, sliced
- Tortilla chips

1. In a small bowl, combine the cream cheese, dressing, sour cream and blue cheese. Transfer to a 3-quart crock pot. Layer with chicken, wing sauce and 1 cup cheese. Cover and cook on low for 2 to 3 hours or until heated through. 2. Sprinkle with remaining cheese and onion. Serve with tortilla chips.

Party Time Artichokes

Prep time: 10 minutes | Cook time: 2½ to 4 hours | Serves 4

- 4 whole, fresh artichokes
- 1 teaspoon salt
- 4 tablespoons lemon juice, divided
- 2 tablespoons butter, melted

1. Wash and trim off the tough outer leaves and around the bottom of the artichokes. Cut off about 1 inch from the tops of each, and trim off the tips of the leaves. Spread the top leaves apart and use a long-handled spoon to pull out the fuzzy chokes in their centers. 2. Stand the prepared artichokes upright in the crock pot. Sprinkle each with ¼ teaspoon salt. 3. Spoon 2 tablespoons lemon juice over the artichokes. Pour in enough water to cover the bottom half of the artichokes. 4. Cover and cook on high for 2½ to 4 hours. 5. Serve with melted butter and remaining lemon juice for dipping.

Chapter ⑧

Vegetables and Sides

Cipollini Onions with Balsamic Glaze

Prep time: 10 minutes | Cook time: 3 to 4 hours | Serves 8

- ½ cup (1 stick) unsalted butter
- ¼ cup firmly packed light brown sugar
- ½ cup balsamic vinegar
- ⅓ cup double-strength chicken broth
- 1½ pounds (680 g) cipollini onions, peeled

1. Put all the ingredients in the insert of a 5- to 7-quart crock pot and stir to coat the onions. 2. Cover and cook on low for 3 to 4 hours, until the onions are tender and glazed with the sauce. 3. Cool and serve at room temperature or store in the refrigerator for up to 4 days.

Barley-Stuffed Cabbage Rolls with Pine Nuts and Currants

Prep time: 20 minutes | Cook time: 6 to 8 hours | Serves 4

- 1 large head green cabbage, cored
- 1 tablespoon olive oil
- 1 large yellow onion, chopped
- 3 cups cooked pearl barley
- 3 ounces (85 g) feta cheese, crumbled
- ½ cup dried currants
- 2 tablespoons pine nuts, toasted
- 2 tablespoons chopped fresh flat-leaf parsley
- ½ teaspoon sea salt
- ½ teaspoon black pepper
- ½ cup apple juice
- 1 tablespoon apple cider vinegar
- 1 (15-ounce / 425-g) can crushed tomatoes, with the juice

1. Steam the cabbage head in a large pot over boiling water for 8 minutes. Remove to a cutting board and let cool slightly. 2. Remove 16 leaves from the cabbage head (reserve the rest of the cabbage for another use). Cut off the raised portion of the center vein of each cabbage leaf (do not cut out the vein). 3. Heat the oil in a large nonstick lidded skillet over medium heat. Add the onion, cover, and cook 6 minutes, or until tender. Remove to a large bowl. 4. Stir the barley, feta cheese, currants, pine nuts, and parsley into the onion mixture. Season with ¼ teaspoon of the salt and ¼ teaspoon of the pepper. 5. Place cabbage leaves on a work surface. On 1 cabbage leaf, spoon about ⅓ cup of the barley mixture into the center. Fold in the edges of the leaf over the barley mixture and roll the cabbage leaf up as if you were making a burrito. Repeat for the remaining 15 cabbage leaves and filling. 6. Arrange the cabbage rolls in the crock pot. 7. Combine the remaining ¼ teaspoon salt, ¼ teaspoon

pepper, the apple juice, apple cider vinegar, and tomatoes. Pour the apple juice mixture evenly over the cabbage rolls. 8. Cover and cook on high 2 hours or on low for 6 to 8 hours. Serve hot.

Sweet Potato Gratin

Prep time: 15 minutes | Cook time: 4 hours | Serves 12

- 1 tablespoon butter, at room temperature
- 1 large sweet onion, such as Vidalia, thinly sliced
- 2 pounds (907 g) sweet potatoes, peeled and thinly sliced
- 1 tablespoon all-purpose flour
- 1 teaspoon chopped fresh thyme
- ½ teaspoon sea salt
- ½ teaspoon black pepper
- 2 ounces (57 g) grated fresh Parmesan cheese
- Nonstick cooking oil spray
- ½ cup vegetable stock

1. Melt the butter in a medium nonstick skillet over medium heat. Add the onion and sauté 5 minutes, or until lightly browned. Remove to a large bowl. 2. Add the sweet potatoes, flour, thyme, salt, pepper, and one-half of the grated Parmesan cheese in the large bowl. Toss gently to coat the sweet potato slices with the flour mixture. 3. Coat the crock pot with cooking oil spray. Transfer the sweet potato mixture to the crock pot. 4. Pour the stock over the mixture. Sprinkle with the remaining Parmesan. Cover and cook on low for 4 hours or until the potatoes are tender. Serve hot.

Black-Eyed Peas and Ham

Prep time: 20 minutes | Cook time: 6 hours | Serves 12

- 1 (16-ounce / 454-g) package dried black-eyed peas, rinsed and sorted
- ½ pound (227 g) fully cooked boneless ham, finely chopped
- 1 medium onion, finely chopped
- 1 medium sweet red pepper, finely chopped
- 5 bacon strips, cooked and crumbled
- 1 large jalapeno pepper,
- seeded and finely chopped
- 2 garlic cloves, minced
- 1½ teaspoons ground cumin
- 1 teaspoon reduced-sodium chicken bouillon granules
- ½ teaspoon salt
- ½ teaspoon cayenne pepper
- ¼ teaspoon pepper
- 6 cups water
- Minced fresh cilantro (optional)
- Hot cooked rice

1. In a 6-quart crock pot, combine the first 13 ingredients. Cover and cook on low for 6 to 8 hours or until peas are tender. Sprinkle with cilantro if desired. Serve with rice.

Cheesy Creamed Corn with Bacon

Prep time: 15 minutes | Cook time: 3 hours | Serves 8

- 12 ears of corn, shucked and cut from the cob, or 2 pounds (907 g) frozen corn kernels
- 2 bacon slices, finely chopped
- 8 ounces (227 g) cream cheese, at room temperature
- 6 ounces (170 g) American cheese, finely diced
- ½ cup whole milk
- 3 ounces (85 g) sour cream
- 3 fresh thyme sprigs
- 2 bay leaves
- ¾ teaspoon kosher salt, plus more for seasoning
- ½ teaspoon freshly ground black pepper, plus more for seasoning

1. In the crock pot, combine the corn, bacon, cream cheese, cheese, milk, sour cream, thyme, and bay leaves. Season with the salt and pepper, and stir to combine. Cover and cook on low for 3 hours, until the corn is cooked and the sauce has thickened slightly. 2. Remove the cover and discard the thyme and bay leaves. Season with additional salt and pepper as needed, and serve.

Zucchini, Tomato, and Leek Gratin

Prep time: 20 minutes | Cook time: 2½ to 3 hours | Serves 6 to 8

- 4 cup shredded zucchini
- 3 teaspoons salt
- 3 medium tomatoes, cut into ½-inch-thick slices
- 2 leeks, coarsely chopped, using the white and tender green parts
- 4 tablespoons extra-virgin olive oil
- 2 teaspoons dried tarragon
- ½ teaspoon freshly ground black pepper
- 2 tablespoons tomato paste
- ½ cup chicken broth
- Freshly grated Parmigiano-Reggiano cheese, for garnish

1. Place the zucchini in a colander, sprinkle with 1 teaspoon of the salt, and press any moisture out of the zucchini. Sprinkle the tomatoes with 1 teaspoon salt and let drain on paper towels. 2. Toss the leeks with 2 tablespoons of the oil and pour the remaining 2 tablespoons oil in the insert of a 5- to 7-quart crock pot. Combine the tarragon, pepper, tomato paste, remaining salt and the broth in a small bowl. Arrange a layer of tomatoes in the slow-cooker insert and sprinkle with 2 tablespoons of the tomato paste mixture. Top with a layer of zucchini, sprinkle with 2 tablespoons of the tomato paste mixture, and top with some of the leeks. Continue to layer the ingredients, and pour the remainder of tomato paste mixture over the vegetables. 3. Cover and cook on high for 1½ to 2 hours, until the vegetables are tender. Remove the cover and cook on low another hour. 4. Serve the gratin warm or at room temperature with a sprinkling of grated Parmigiano-Reggiano.

Broccoli Delight

Prep time: 15 minutes | Cook time: 2 to 6 hours | Serves 4 to 6

- 1 to 2 pounds (454 to 907 g) broccoli, chopped
- 2 cups cauliflower, chopped
- 1 (10¾-ounce / 305-g) can 98% fat-free cream of celery soup
- ½ teaspoon salt
- ¼ teaspoon black pepper
- 1 medium onion, diced
- 2 to 4 garlic cloves, crushed, according to your taste preference
- ½ cup vegetable broth

1. Combine all ingredients in crock pot. 2. Cook on low 4 to 6 hours, or on high 2 to 3 hours.

Glazed Maple Sweet Potatoes

Prep time: 10 minutes | Cook time: 7 to 9 hours | Serves 5

- 5 medium sweet potatoes, cut in ½-inch-thick slices
- ¼ cup brown sugar, packed
- ¼ cup pure maple syrup
- ¼ cup apple cider
- 2 tablespoons butter

1. Place potatoes in crock pot. 2. In a small bowl, combine brown sugar, maple syrup, and apple cider. Mix well. Pour over potatoes. Stir until all potato slices are covered. 3. Cover and cook on low 7 to 9 hours, or until potatoes are tender. 4. Stir in butter before serving.

Stuffed Mushrooms

Prep time: 20 minutes | Cook time: 2 to 4 hours | Serves 4 to 6

- 8 to 10 large mushrooms
- ¼ teaspoon minced garlic
- 1 tablespoon oil
- Dash of salt
- Dash of pepper
- Dash of cayenne pepper (optional)
- ¼ cup shredded Monterey Jack cheese

1. Remove stems from mushrooms and dice. 2. Heat oil in skillet. Sauté diced stems with garlic until softened. Remove skillet from heat. 3. Stir in seasonings and cheese. Stuff into mushroom shells. Place in crock pot. 4. Cover. Heat on low 2 to 4 hours.

Creamed Kale

Prep time: 20 minutes | Cook time: 3 hours | Serves 8

- Cooking spray or 1 tablespoon extra-virgin olive oil
- ½ stick unsalted butter
- 2 garlic cloves, minced
- ½ cup heavy (whipping) cream
- 2 ounces (57 g) cream cheese
- 1½ cups whole milk
- 1 cup low-sodium chicken stock
- 4 tablespoons all-purpose flour
- ½ cup finely grated Parmesan cheese
- ½ teaspoon kosher salt, plus more for seasoning
- ½ teaspoon freshly ground black pepper, plus more for seasoning
- ¼ teaspoon ground nutmeg
- ¼ teaspoon red pepper flakes
- 2 bunches kale, washed, stemmed, and leaves torn

1. If using a crock pot with a stove-top function to make the sauce, first use the cooking spray or olive oil to coat the inside (bottom and sides) of the crock pot. In the crock pot or in a Dutch oven or heavy-bottomed pan over medium-high heat, prepare the sauce by whisking together the butter, garlic, whipping cream, cream cheese, milk, chicken stock, flour, and Parmesan until the butter and cheese are melted and the flour is incorporated, and the sauce is free of lumps. 2. If you prepared the sauce outside the crock pot, use the cooking spray or olive oil to coat the inside (bottom and sides) of the crock pot. Add the sauce to the crock pot, along with the salt, pepper, nutmeg, red pepper flakes, and kale. Stir to combine. Cover and cook on low for 3 hours. 3. Season with additional salt and pepper, as needed. Serve.

Spinach Parmesan Strata

Prep time: 15 minutes | Cook time: 3 to 3½ hours | Serves 6 to 8

- 2 tablespoons unsalted butter
- 2 medium shallots, finely chopped
- 2 (16-ounce / 454-g) packages frozen chopped spinach, defrosted and drained
- ¼ teaspoon freshly grated nutmeg
- 6 large eggs
- 2 cups milk
- 1½ teaspoons salt
- 1 teaspoon Tabasco sauce
- 6 cups bread cubes, crusts removed (a sturdy bread like Pepperidge Farm)
- 1 cup freshly grated Parmesan cheese

1. Coat the inside of the insert of a 5- to 7-quart crock pot with nonstick cooking spray or line it with a slow-cooker liner according to the manufacturer's directions. 2. Melt the butter in a medium skillet over medium-high heat. Add the shallots and sauté for 2 minutes, until softened. Add the spinach and nutmeg and sauté until the liquid in the pan is evaporated. Set aside to cool. 3. Whisk together the eggs, milk, salt and Tabasco in a large bowl. Arrange half the bread in the slow-cooker insert. Top with half of the spinach mixture and half the cheese. Layer the remaining bread, spinach, and cheese. Pour the egg mixture over the casserole and press down to make sure the bread has absorbed the egg mixture. Cover and cook on low for 3 to 3½ hours, until the strata is cooked through. 4. Serve from the cooker set on warm.

Eggplant and Zucchini Casserole

Prep time: 20 minutes | Cook time: 5 to 6 hours | Serves 6

- 2 egg whites
- 1 medium eggplant
- 1 medium zucchini
- 1½ cups bread crumbs
- 1 teaspoon garlic powder
- 1 teaspoon low-sodium Italian seasoning
- 1 (48-ounce / 1.4-kg) jar fat-free, low-sodium spaghetti sauce
- 1 (8-ounce / 227-g) bag low-fat shredded Mozzarella cheese

1. Beat egg whites in small bowl. 2. Slice eggplant and zucchini. Place in separate bowl. 3. Combine in another bowl bread crumbs, garlic powder, and Italian seasoning. 4. Dip sliced veggies in egg white and then in bread crumbs. Layer in crock pot, pouring sauce and sprinkling cheese over each layer. (Reserve ½ cup cheese). Top with sauce. 5. Cover. Cook on low 5 to 6 hours, or until vegetables are tender. 6. Top with remaining cheese during last 15 minutes of cooking.

Purely Artichokes

Prep time: 15 minutes | Cook time: 6 to 8 hours | Serves 4 to 6

- 4 to 6 artichokes
- 1 to 1½ teaspoons salt
- 1 cup lemon juice, divided
- 2 cups hot water
- 1 stick (½ cup) butter, melted

1. Wash and trim artichokes. Cut off about 1 inch from top. If you wish, trim tips of leaves. Stand chokes upright in crock pot. 2. Sprinkle each choke with ¼ teaspoon salt and 2 tablespoons lemon juice. 3. Pour 2 cups hot water around the base of the artichokes. 4. Cover and cook on low 6 to 8 hours. 5. Serve with melted butter and lemon juice for dipping.

Refrigerator Mashed Potatoes

Prep time: 30 minutes | Cook time: 2 hours | Serves 8 to 10

- 5 pounds (2.3 kg) potatoes
- 1 (8-ounce / 227-g) package cream cheese, softened
- 1 cup sour cream
- 1 teaspoon salt
- ¼ teaspoon pepper
- ¼ cup crisp bacon, crumbled
- 2 tablespoons butter

1. Cook and mash potatoes. 2. Add remaining ingredients except butter. Put in crock pot. Dot with butter. 3. Cover. Cook on low 2 hours.

Lemon-Rosemary Beets

Prep time: 10 minutes | Cook time: 8 hours | Serves 7

- 2 pounds (907 g) beets, peeled and cut into wedges
- 2 tablespoons fresh lemon juice
- 2 tablespoons extra-virgin olive oil
- 2 tablespoons honey
- 1 tablespoon apple cider vinegar
- ¾ teaspoon sea salt
- ½ teaspoon black pepper
- 2 sprigs fresh rosemary
- ½ teaspoon lemon zest

1. Place the beets in the crock pot. 2. Whisk the lemon juice, extra-virgin olive oil, honey, apple cider vinegar, salt, and pepper together in a small bowl. Pour over the beets. 3. Add the sprigs of rosemary to the crock pot. 4. Cover and cook on low for 8 hours, or until the beets are tender. 5. Remove and discard the rosemary sprigs. Stir in the lemon zest. Serve hot.

Green Beans with Bacon and Tomatoes

Prep time: 15 minutes | Cook time: 4½ hours | Serves 12

- 1 (14-ounce / 397-g) package thick-sliced bacon strips, chopped
- 1 large red onion, chopped
- 2 (16-ounce / 454-g) packages frozen cut green beans
- 1 (28-ounce / 794-g) can petite diced tomatoes,
- undrained
- ¼ cup packed brown sugar
- 1 tablespoon seasoned pepper
- ½ teaspoon seasoned salt
- 1 (16-ounce / 454-g) can red beans, rinsed and drained

1. In a large skillet, cook bacon over medium heat until partially cooked but not crisp, stirring occasionally. Remove with a slotted spoon; drain on paper towels. Discard drippings, reserving 2 tablespoons. Add onion to drippings; cook and stir over medium-high heat until tender. 2. In a 4- or 5-quart crock pot, combine green beans, tomatoes, brown sugar, pepper, salt, bacon and onion. Cook, covered, on low 4 hours. Stir in red beans. Cook 30 minutes longer or until heated through.

Dried Corn

Prep time: 5 minutes | Cook time: 4 hours | Serves 4

- 1 (15-ounce / 425-g) can dried corn
- 2 tablespoons sugar
- 3 tablespoons butter,
- softened
- 1 teaspoon salt
- 1 cup half-and-half
- 2 tablespoons water

1. Place all ingredients in crock pot. Mix together well. 2. Cover and cook on low 4 hours. 3. Serve.

Hominy and Ham

Prep time: 10 minutes | Cook time: 1½ to 3 hours | Serves 12 to 14

- 3 (29-ounce / 822-g) cans hominy, drained
- 1 (10¾-ounce / 305-g) can cream of chicken soup
- ½ pound (227 g) Cheddar
- cheese, shredded or cubed
- 1 pound (454 g) cubed cooked ham
- 2 (2¼-ounce / 64-g) cans green chilies, undrained

1. Mix all ingredients together in crock pot. 2. Cover and cook on high for 1½ hours, or on low for 2 to 3 hours, or until bubbly and cheese is melted.

Tomato, Corn, and Yellow Squash with Dill Butter

Prep time: 10 minutes | Cook time: 1½ to 2 hours | Serves 6 to 8

- ½ cup (1 stick) unsalted butter, melted
- 1 teaspoon salt
- ½ teaspoon freshly ground black pepper
- 2 tablespoons finely
- chopped fresh dill
- 6 cups fresh corn kernels (6 to 8 medium ears)
- 2 cups cherry tomatoes
- 4 yellow squash, cut into ½-inch pieces

1. Combine all the ingredients in the insert of a 5- to 7-quart crock pot. Cover and cook on high for 1½ to 2 hours, until the corn and tomatoes are tender. 2. Serve from the crock pot set on warm.

Squash Medley

Prep time: 20 minutes | Cook time: 4 to 6 hours | Serves 8

- 8 summer squash, each about 4-inches long, thinly sliced
- ½ teaspoon salt
- 2 tomatoes, peeled and chopped
- ¼ cup sliced green onions
- Half a small sweet green
- pepper, chopped
- 1 chicken bouillon cube
- ¼ cup hot water
- 4 slices bacon, fried and crumbled
- ¼ cup fine dry bread crumbs

1. Sprinkle squash with salt. 2. In crock pot, layer half the squash, tomatoes, onions, and pepper. Repeat layers. 3. Dissolve bouillon in hot water. Pour into crock pot. 4. Top with bacon. Sprinkle bread crumbs over top. 5. Cover. Cook on low 4 to 6 hours.

Greek-Style Green Beans

Prep time: 5 minutes | Cook time: 2 to 5 hours | Serves 6

- 20 ounces (567 g) whole or cut-up frozen green beans (not French cut)
- 2 cups tomato sauce
- 2 teaspoons dried onion
- flakes (optional)
- Pinch of dried marjoram or oregano
- Pinch of ground nutmeg
- Pinch of cinnamon

1. Combine all ingredients in crock pot, mixing together thoroughly. 2. Cover and cook on low 2 to 4 hours if the beans are defrosted, or 3 to 5 hours on low if the beans are frozen, or until the beans are done to your liking.

Easy Beans and Potatoes with Bacon

Prep time: 15 minutes | Cook time: 6 hours | Serves 10

- 8 bacon strips, chopped
- 1½ pounds (680 g) fresh green beans, trimmed and cut into 2-inch pieces (about 4 cups)
- 4 medium potatoes, peeled and cubed (½ inch)
- 1 small onion, halved and sliced
- ¼ cup reduced-sodium chicken broth
- ½ teaspoon salt
- ¼ teaspoon pepper

1. In a large skillet, cook bacon over medium heat until crisp, stirring occasionally. Remove to paper towels with a slotted spoon; drain, reserving 1 tablespoon drippings. Cover and refrigerate bacon until serving. 2. In a 5-quart crock pot, combine the remaining ingredients; stir in reserved drippings. Cover and cook on low for 6 to 8 hours or until potatoes are tender. Stir in bacon; heat through.

Caramelized Onions

Prep time: 10 minutes | Cook time: 12 hours | Serves 6 to 8

- 6 to 8 large Vidalia or other sweet onions
- 4 tablespoons butter, or
- margarine
- 1 (10-ounce / 283-g) can chicken or vegetable broth

1. Peel onions. Remove stems and root ends. Place in crock pot. 2. Pour butter and broth over. 3. Cook on low 12 hours.

Orange Yams

Prep time: 15 minutes | Cook time: 3 hours | Serves 6 to 8

- 1 (40-ounce / 1.1-kg) can yams, drained
- 2 apples, cored, peeled, thinly sliced
- 3 tablespoons butter, melted
- 2 teaspoons orange zest
- 1 cup orange juice
- 2 tablespoons cornstarch
- ½ cup brown sugar
- 1 teaspoon salt
- Dash of ground cinnamon and/or nutmeg

1. Place yams and apples in crock pot. 2. Add butter and orange zest. 3. Combine remaining ingredients and pour over yams. 4. Cover. Cook on high 1 hour and on low 2 hours, or until apples are tender.

Savory Butternut Squash and Apples

Prep time: 10 minutes | Cook time: 4 hours | Serves 10

- 1 (3-pound / 1.4-kg) butternut squash, peeled, seeded, and cubed
- 4 cooking apples (Granny Smith or Honeycrisp), peeled, cored, and chopped
- ¾ cup dried currants
- ½ sweet yellow onion such as Vidalia, sliced thin
- 1 tablespoon ground cinnamon
- 1½ teaspoons ground nutmeg

1. Combine the squash, apples, currants, and onion in the crock pot. Sprinkle with the cinnamon and nutmeg. 2. Cook on high for 4 hours, or until the squash is tender and cooked through. Stir occasionally while cooking.

"Baked" Tomatoes

Prep time: 5 minutes | Cook time: ¾ to 1 hour | Serves 4

- 2 tomatoes, each cut in half
- ½ tablespoon olive oil
- ½ teaspoon parsley, chopped, or ¼ teaspoon dry
- parsley flakes
- ¼ teaspoon dried oregano
- ¼ teaspoon dried basil
- Nonfat cooking spray

1. Place tomato halves in crock pot sprayed with nonfat cooking spray. 2. Drizzle oil over tomatoes. Sprinkle with remaining ingredients. 3. Cover. Cook on high 45 minutes to 1 hour.

Cheesy Corn

Prep time: 10 minutes | Cook time: 4 hours | Serves 10

- 3 (16-ounce / 454-g) packages frozen corn
- 1 (8-ounce / 227-g) package cream cheese, cubed
- ¼ cup butter, cubed
- 3 tablespoons water
- 3 tablespoons milk
- 2 tablespoons sugar
- 6 slices American cheese, cut into squares

1. Combine all ingredients in crock pot. Mix well. 2. Cover. Cook on low 4 hours, or until heated through and the cheese is melted.

Potatoes Boulangerie

Prep time: 20 minutes | Cook time: 2½ to 3 hours | Serves 6 to 8

- 6 medium russet potatoes, peeled and cut into ¼-inch-thick slices
- 6 strips bacon, cut into ½-inch pieces
- 3 leeks, thinly sliced, using the white and some of the
- tender green parts
- 2 teaspoons dried thyme
- 1 cup double-strength chicken broth
- 1½ teaspoons salt
- 1 teaspoon Tabasco sauce
- 1 cup heavy cream

1. Coat the insert of a 5- to 7-quart crock pot with nonstick cooking spray or line it with a slow-cooker liner according to the manufacturer's directions. Arrange the potatoes in the cooker and set aside. 2. Cook the bacon in a large skillet until crisp, then transfer to paper towels to drain. Cook the leeks and thyme in the bacon drippings until the leeks are soft, 2 to 3 minutes. 3. Add the chicken broth, salt, and Tabasco to the skillet and heat, scraping up any browned bits from the bottom of the pan. Pour the contents of the skillet over the potatoes and pour the heavy cream evenly over the potatoes. Cover and cook on high for 2½ to 3 hours, until the potatoes are tender. 4. Serve from the crock pot set on warm.

Balsamic Collard Greens

Prep time: 20 minutes | Cook time: 4 hours | Serves 5

- 3 bacon slices
- 1 cup chopped sweet onion
- 1 pound (454 g) fresh collard greens, rinsed, stemmed, and chopped
- ¼ teaspoon sea salt
- 2 garlic cloves, minced
- 1 bay leaf
- 2 cups vegetable or chicken stock
- 3 tablespoons balsamic vinegar
- 1 tablespoon honey

1. Cook bacon in a medium skillet over medium heat until crisp, about 6 minutes. Remove the bacon to a paper towel–lined plate to cool. Crumble the bacon. 2. Add the onion to bacon drippings and cook for 5 minutes, or until tender. 3. Add the collard greens and cook 2 to 3 minutes or until the greens begin to wilt, stirring occasionally. 4. Place the collard greens, salt, garlic, bay leaf, and stock in the crock pot. Cover and cook on low for 3½ to 4 hours. 5. Combine the balsamic vinegar and honey in a small bowl. Stir the vinegar mixture into the collard greens just before serving. Serve hot, sprinkled with the crumbled bacon.

Rustic Potatoes au Gratin

Prep time: 10 minutes | Cook time: 6 to 8 hours | Serves 6

- ½ cup skim milk
- 1 (10¾-ounce / 305-g) can light condensed Cheddar cheese soup
- 1 (8-ounce / 227-g) package fat-free cream cheese, softened
- 1 clove garlic, minced
- ¼ teaspoon ground nutmeg
- ¼ teaspoon black pepper
- 2 pounds (907 g) baking potatoes, cut into ¼-inch-thick slices
- 1 small onion, thinly sliced
- Paprika
- Nonfat cooking spray

1. Heat milk in small saucepan over medium heat until small bubbles form around edge of pan. Remove from heat. 2. Add soup, cream cheese, garlic, nutmeg, and pepper to pan. Stir until smooth. 3. Spray inside of crock pot with nonfat cooking spray. Layer one-quarter of potatoes and onions on bottom of crock pot. 4. Top with one-quarter of soup mixture. Repeat layers 3 times. 5. Cover. Cook on low 6 to 8 hours, or until potatoes are tender and most of liquid is absorbed. 6. Sprinkle with paprika before serving.

Sweet-Sour Cabbage

Prep time: 20 minutes | Cook time: 3 to 5 hours | Serves 6

- 1 medium head red or green cabbage, shredded
- 2 onions, chopped
- 4 tart apples, pared, quartered
- ½ cup raisins
- ¼ cup lemon juice
- ¼ cup cider, or apple juice
- 3 tablespoons honey
- 1 tablespoon caraway seeds
- ⅛ teaspoon allspice
- ½ teaspoon salt

1. Combine all ingredients in crock pot. 2. Cook on high 3 to 5 hours, depending upon how crunchy or soft you want the cabbage and onions.

Zippy Vegetable Medley

Prep time: 15 minutes | Cook time: 2½ hours | Serves 4 to 5

- 1 (16-ounce / 454-g) package frozen broccoli, cauliflower, and carrots
- 1 (16-ounce / 454-g) package frozen corn
- 2 (10½-ounce / 298-g) cans fiesta nacho cheese soup
- ½ cup milk

1. Combine broccoli mixture and corn in crock pot. 2. Combine soups and milk in a microwave-safe bowl. Microwave for 1 minute on high, or just enough to mix well. When blended, pour over vegetables. 3. Cover and cook on high 2½ hours, or until hot and bubbly and vegetables are done to your liking.

Bacon and Sausage Stuffing

Prep time: 25 minutes | Cook time: 4 hours | Serves 20

- 1 pound (454 g) bulk pork sausage
- 1 pound (454 g) thick-sliced bacon strips, chopped
- ½ cup butter, cubed
- 1 large onion, chopped
- 3 celery ribs, sliced
- 10½ cups unseasoned stuffing cubes
- 1 cup sliced fresh mushrooms
- 1 cup chopped fresh parsley
- 4 teaspoons dried sage leaves
- 4 teaspoons dried thyme
- 6 eggs
- 2 (10¾-ounce / 305-g) cans condensed cream of chicken soup, undiluted
- 1¼ cups chicken stock

1. In a large skillet, cook sausage over medium heat for 6 to 8 minutes or until no longer pink, breaking into crumbles. Remove with a slotted spoon; drain on paper towels. Discard drippings. 2. Add bacon to pan; cook over medium heat until crisp. Remove to paper towels to drain. Discard drippings.

Wipe out pan. In same pan, heat butter over medium-high heat. Add onion and celery; cook and stir 6 to 8 minutes or until tender. Remove from heat. 3. In a large bowl, combine stuffing cubes, sausage, bacon, onion mixture, mushrooms, parsley, sage and thyme. In a small bowl, whisk eggs, soup and stock; pour over stuffing mixture and toss to coat. 4. Transfer to a greased 6-quart crock pot. Cook, covered, on low 4 to 5 hours or until a thermometer reads 160°F (71°C). Remove lid; let stand 15 minutes before serving.

Apple Praline Sweet Potato Gratin

Prep time: 20 minutes | Cook time: 7 hours | Serves 6 to 8

- 4 large sweet potatoes, peeled and cut into ½-inch-thick slices
- 2 large Granny Smith apples, peeled, cored, and cut into ½-inch-thick slices
- ½ cup (1 stick) unsalted butter, melted
- ½ cup firmly packed light brown sugar
- ¼ cup dark corn syrup
- ½ cup apple cider or apple juice
- 1 teaspoon ground cinnamon
- 1 cup pecans, toasted, for garnish

1. Coat the insert of a 5- to 7-quart crock pot with nonstick cooking spray or line it with a slow-cooker liner according to the manufacturer's directions. 2. Layer the sweet potatoes and apples in the crock pot. Combine all the remaining ingredients except the pecans in a small mixing bowl and pour over the potatoes and apples in the cooker. Cover and cook on low for 7 hours, until the potatoes are tender when pierced with the tip of a paring knife. 3. Sprinkle the top of the casserole with the pecans. Serve from the cooker set on warm.

Glazed Root Vegetable Medley

Prep time: 20 minutes | Cook time: 3 hours | Serves 6

- 2 medium parsnips
- 4 medium carrots
- 1 turnip, about 4½ inches around
- ½ cup water
- 1 teaspoon salt
- ½ cup sugar
- 3 tablespoons butter
- ½ teaspoon salt

1. Clean and peel vegetables. Cut in 1-inch pieces. 2. Dissolve salt in water in saucepan. Add vegetables and boil for 10 minutes. Drain, reserving ½ cup liquid. 3. Place vegetables in crock pot. Add liquid. 4. Stir in sugar, butter, and salt. 5. Cover. Cook on low 3 hours.

All-American Stewed Tomatoes

Prep time: 15 minutes | Cook time: 8 hours | Serves 6 to 8

- 2 tablespoons olive oil
- 1 medium onion, coarsely chopped
- 1 medium green bell pepper, seeded and coarsely chopped
- 10 large tomatoes, peeled, cored, and cut into wedges
- 3 tablespoons brown sugar
- 1½ teaspoons salt
- ½ teaspoon freshly ground black pepper

1. Combine all the ingredients in the insert of a 5- to 7-quart crock pot. Cover and cook on low for 8 hours, until the tomatoes are tender. 2. Allow the tomatoes to cool before serving.

Summer Vegetable Mélange

Prep time: 15 minutes | Cook time: 6 hours | Serves 6

- ½ cup extra-virgin olive oil
- ¼ cup balsamic vinegar
- 1 tablespoon dried basil
- 1 teaspoon dried thyme
- ¼ teaspoon salt
- 2 cups cauliflower florets
- 2 zucchini, diced into 1-inch pieces
- 1 yellow bell pepper, cut into strips
- 1 cup halved button mushrooms

1. In a large bowl, whisk together the oil, vinegar, basil, thyme, and salt, until blended. 2. Add the cauliflower, zucchini, bell pepper, and mushrooms, and toss to coat. 3. Transfer the vegetables to the insert of a crock pot. 4. Cover and cook on low for 6 hours. 5. Serve.

Kale with Bacon

Prep time: 15 minutes | Cook time: 6 hours | Serves 8

- 2 tablespoons bacon fat
- 2 pounds (907 g) kale, rinsed and chopped roughly
- 12 bacon slices, cooked and chopped
- 2 teaspoons minced garlic
- 2 cups vegetable broth
- Salt, for seasoning
- Freshly ground black pepper, for seasoning

1. Generously grease the insert of the crock pot with the bacon fat. 2. Add the kale, bacon, garlic, and broth to the insert. Gently toss to mix. 3. Cover and cook on low for 6 hours. 4. Season with salt and pepper, and serve hot.

Sweet Potato, Fruit Compote

Prep time: 20 minutes | Cook time: 5 to 6 hours | Serves 8

- 4 cups sweet potatoes, peeled and cubed
- 3 tart cooking apples, peeled and diced
- 1 (20-ounce / 567-g)
- unsweetened pineapple chunks, undrained
- ¼ cup brown sugar
- 1 cup miniature marshmallows, divided

1. Cook sweet potatoes in a small amount of water in a saucepan until almost soft. Drain. 2. Combine sweet potatoes, apples, and pineapples in crock pot. 3. Sprinkle with brown sugar and ⅔ cup marshmallows. 4. Cover. Cook on low 5 to 6 hours. 5. Thirty minutes before serving, top potatoes and fruit with remaining ⅓ cup marshmallows. Cover and continue cooking.

Vegetable Curry

Prep time: 15 minutes | Cook time: 3 to 10 hours | Serves 8 to 10

- 1 (16-ounce / 454-g) package baby carrots
- 3 medium potatoes, cubed
- 1 pound (454 g) fresh or frozen green beans, cut in 2-inch pieces
- 1 green pepper, chopped
- 1 onion, chopped
- 1 to 2 cloves garlic, minced
- 1 (15-ounce / 425-g) can garbanzo beans, drained
- 1 (28-ounce / 794-g) can crushed tomatoes
- 3 tablespoons minute tapioca
- 3 teaspoons curry powder
- 2 teaspoons salt
- 1¾ cups boiling water
- 2 teaspoons chicken bouillon granules, or 2 chicken bouillon cubes

1. Combine carrots, potatoes, green beans, pepper, onion, garlic, garbanzo beans, and crushed tomatoes in large bowl. 2. Stir in tapioca, curry powder, and salt. 3. Dissolve bouillon in boiling water. Pour over vegetables. Mix well. Spoon into large cooker, or two medium-sized ones. 4. Cover. Cook on low 8 to 10 hours, or on high 3 to 4 hours. Serve.

Chapter 9

Desserts

Carmeled Pears 'n Wine

Prep time: 10 minutes | Cook time: 4 to 6 hours | Serves 6

- 6 medium fresh pears with stems
- 1 cup white wine
- ½ cup sugar
- ½ cup water
- 3 tablespoons lemon juice
- 2 apple cinnamon sticks,
- each about 2½ to 3 inch long
- 3 whole dried cloves
- ¼ teaspoon ground nutmeg
- 6 tablespoons fat-free caramel apple dip

1. Peel pears, leaving whole with stems intact. 2. Place upright in crock pot. Shave bottom if needed to level fruit. 3. Combine wine, sugar, water, lemon juice, cinnamon, cloves, and nutmeg. Pour over pears. 4. Cook on low 4 to 6 hours, or until pears are tender. 5. Cool pears in liquid. 6. Transfer pears to individual serving dishes. Place 2 teaspoons cooking liquid in bottom of each dish. 7. Microwave caramel dip for 20 seconds and stir. Repeat until heated through. 8. Drizzle caramel over pears and serve.

Cherries Jubilee Lava Cake

Prep time: 20 minutes | Cook time: 2 hours | Serves 4 to 6

- Cherries:
- 2 (16-ounce / 454-g) bags frozen unsweetened pitted sweet cherries, defrosted and drained
- ¼ cup sugar
- 2 tablespoons cornstarch
- 2 tablespoons brandy or Grand Marnier
- Chocolate Cake:
- ½ cup milk
- 3 tablespoons unsalted
- butter, melted
- 1 teaspoon vanilla bean paste
- 1 cup granulated sugar
- 1 cup all-purpose flour
- ½ cup cocoa powder (make sure to use natural cocoa powder, not Dutch process)
- 2 teaspoons baking powder
- ¾ cup firmly packed light brown sugar
- 1¼ cups boiling water

1. Coat the insert for a 3½- to 4-quart crock pot with nonstick cooking spray. Add all the cherries, sugar, cornstarch, and brandy to the slow-cooker insert and stir to combine. 2. Stir together the milk, butter, and vanilla bean paste in a mixing bowl. Gradually stir in the granulated sugar, flour, ¼ cup of the cocoa powder, and the baking powder. 3. Spread the batter evenly over the cherries in the slow-cooker insert. Mix together the brown sugar and remaining ¼ cup cocoa powder in a small bowl and sprinkle evenly over the batter. Pour in the boiling water (do not stir). 4. Cover and cook on high for 2 hours, until a skewer inserted into the center comes out clean. Uncover and allow to cool for about 20 minutes. 5. Serve spooned from the crock pot, so the cherries are a surprise resting on top of the cake.

Cranberry Pudding

Prep time: 20 minutes | Cook time: 3 to 4 hours | Serves 8 to 10

- Pudding:
- 1⅓ cups flour
- ½ teaspoon salt
- 2 teaspoons baking soda
- ⅓ cup boiling water
- ½ cup dark molasses
- 2 cups whole cranberries
- ½ cup chopped nuts
- ½ cup water
- Butter Sauce:
- 1 cup confectioners sugar
- ½ cup heavy cream or evaporated milk
- ½ cup butter
- 1 teaspoon vanilla

1. Mix together flour and salt. 2. Dissolve soda in boiling water. Add to flour and salt. 3. Stir in molasses. Blend well. 4. Fold in cranberries and nuts. 5. Pour into well greased and floured bread or cake pan that will sit in your cooker. Cover with greased foil. 6. Pour ½ cup water into cooker. Place foil-covered pan in cooker. Cover with cooker lid and steam on high 3 to 4 hours, or until pudding tests done with a wooden pick. 7. Remove pan and uncover. Let stand 5 minutes, then unmold. 8. To make butter sauce, mix together all ingredients in saucepan. Cook, stirring over medium heat until sugar dissolves.

Stewed Figs in Port Wine with Point Reyes Blue Cheese

Prep time: 10 minutes | Cook time: 1½ to 2 hours | Serves 6

- 1½ cups Ruby Port
- 1 cup firmly packed light brown sugar
- 2 whole cloves
- 12 fresh figs
- 1½ cups crumbled Point Reyes blue cheese
- 1 cup chopped toasted walnuts

1. Combine the port, sugar, and cloves in the insert of a 5- to 7-quart crock pot. Add the figs stem-end up to the slow-cooker insert and spoon some of the syrup over the figs. Cover and cook on low for 1½ to 2 hours. Allow the figs to cool in the syrup for 1 hour. 2. Remove the figs to a serving platter. Strain the syrup through a fine-mesh sieve into a saucepan and boil for 5 to 10 minutes until it is thickened. Allow the syrup to cool slightly. 3. Arrange 2 figs in a pool of the syrup on each plate. Sprinkle with the crumbled blue cheese and toasted walnuts before serving.

Just Peachy

Prep time: 5 minutes | Cook time: 4 to 5 hours | Serves 4 to 6

- 4 cups sliced peaches, fresh or canned (if using canned peaches, reserve the juice)
- ⅔ cup rolled dry oats
- ⅓ cup all-purpose baking mix
- ½ cup sugar
- ½ cup brown sugar
- ½ teaspoon cinnamon (optional)
- ½ cup water or reserved peach juice
- Nonstick cooking spray

1. Spray inside of crock pot with nonstick cooking spray. 2. Place peaches in crock pot. 3. In a bowl, mix together all dry ingredients. When blended, stir in water or juice until well mixed. 4. Spoon batter into cooker and stir into peaches, just until blended. 5. Cover and cook on low 4 to 5 hours. 6. Serve warm.

Chocolate Peanut Butter Cake

Prep time: 10 minutes | Cook time: 2 to 2½ hours | Serves 8 to 10

- 2 cups dry milk chocolate cake mix
- ½ cup water
- 6 tablespoons peanut butter
- 2 eggs
- ½ cup chopped nuts

1. Combine all ingredients in electric mixer bowl. Beat for 2 minutes. 2. Spray interior of a baking insert, designed to fit into your crock pot. Flour interior of greased insert. Pour batter into insert. Place insert in crock pot. 3. Cover insert with 8 paper towels. 4. Cover cooker. Cook on high 2 to 2½ hours, or until toothpick inserted into center of cake comes out clean. 5. Allow cake to cool. Then invert onto a serving plate, cut, and serve.

Coconut Jasmine Rice Pudding

Prep time: 15 minutes | Cook time: 2½ to 3 hours | Serves 8

- 2 cups whole milk
- 1 cup sugar
- 2 cups heavy cream
- 4 large eggs, beaten
- 1 teaspoon ground cinnamon
- 1½ cups Jasmine rice,
- rinsed with cold water and drained
- 2 cups shredded coconut, toasted
- Whipped cream, cinnamon sugar, or chopped mangoes and pineapple, for garnish

1. Coat the insert of a 5- to 7-quart crock pot with nonstick cooking spray. Heat the milk in a small saucepan until small bubbles form at the edges of the pan. Remove from the heat. Add the sugar and whisk until dissolved. Whisk together the sweetened milk, cream, eggs, and cinnamon in a mixing bowl. Stir in the rice. Transfer the mixture to the slow-cooker insert. 2. Cover and cook on low for 2½ to 3 hours, until the pudding is set. Remove the cover, stir in the coconut, and cook covered for an additional 30 minutes. Allow the pudding to cool in the insert, then transfer it to a bowl. Cover with plastic wrap and refrigerate until cold. 3. Scoop the pudding into bowls and garnish with whipped cream.

Tender Pound Cake

Prep time: 10 minutes | Cook time: 5 to 6 hours | Serves 8

- 1 tablespoon coconut oil
- 2 cups almond flour
- 1 cup granulated erythritol
- ½ teaspoon cream of tartar
- Pinch salt
- 1 cup butter, melted
- 5 eggs
- 2 teaspoons pure vanilla extract

1. Lightly grease an 8-by-4-inch loaf pan with the coconut oil. 2. In a large bowl, stir together the almond flour, erythritol, cream of tartar, and salt, until well mixed. 3. In a small bowl, whisk together the butter, eggs, and vanilla. 4. Add the wet ingredients to the dry ingredients and stir to combine. 5. Transfer the batter to the loaf pan. 6. Place the loaf pan in the insert of the crock pot. 7. Cover and cook until a toothpick inserted in the center comes out clean, about 5 to 6 hours on low. 8. Serve warm.

Upside-Down Chocolate Pudding Cake

Prep time: 15 minutes | Cook time: 2 to 3 hours | Serves 8

- 1 cup dry all-purpose baking mix
- 1 cup sugar, divided
- 3 tablespoons unsweetened cocoa powder, plus ⅓ cup,
- divided
- ½ cup milk
- 1 teaspoon vanilla
- 1⅔ cups hot water
- Nonstick cooking spray

1. Spray inside of crock pot with nonstick cooking spray. 2. In a bowl, mix together baking mix, ½ cup sugar, 3 tablespoons cocoa powder, milk, and vanilla. Spoon batter evenly into crock pot. 3. In a clean bowl, mix remaining ½ cup sugar, ⅓ cup cocoa powder, and hot water together. Pour over batter in crock pot. Do not stir. 4. Cover and cook on high 2 to 3 hours, or until toothpick inserted in center of cake comes out clean.

Caramel Apples

Prep time: 15 minutes | Cook time: 4 to 6 hours | Serves 4

- 4 very large tart apples, cored
- ½ cup apple juice
- 8 tablespoons brown sugar
- 12 hot cinnamon candies
- 4 tablespoons butter
- 8 caramel candies
- ¼ teaspoon ground cinnamon
- Whipped cream

1. Remove ½-inch-wide strip of peel off the top of each apple and place apples in crock pot. 2. Pour apple juice over apples. 3. Fill the center of each apple with 2 tablespoons brown sugar, 3 hot cinnamon candies, 1 tablespoon butter, and 2 caramel candies. Sprinkle with cinnamon. 4. Cover and cook on low 4 to 6 hours, or until tender. 5. Serve hot with whipped cream.

Blueberry Cornmeal Buckle

Prep time: 25 minutes | Cook time: 3½ hours | Serves 6 to 8

- Nonstick baking spray
- Batter:
- 1¼ cups all-purpose flour
- ¾ cup fine yellow cornmeal
- 1½ teaspoons baking powder
- ¼ teaspoon baking soda
- 2 teaspoon coarse salt
- ½ cup (1 stick) unsalted butter, room temperature
- 1 cup granulated sugar
- 2 teaspoon vanilla extract
- 2 large eggs
- ¾ cup buttermilk, preferably full-fat
- 1 cup blueberries
- Streusel:
- ½ cup all-purpose flour
- 3 tablespoons light brown sugar
- 3 tablespoons unsalted butter, room temperature
- ½ teaspoon ground cinnamon

1. Lightly coat the insert of a 4-quart crock pot with baking spray. Line bottom with parchment and spray. Make the Batter: 2. Whisk together flour, cornmeal, baking powder, baking soda, and salt in a bowl. With an electric mixer on medium, beat butter, sugar, and vanilla until pale and fluffy, 3 to 5 minutes. Beat in eggs, one at a time. Add flour mixture in three batches, alternating with buttermilk; beat until combined. 3. Transfer batter to crock pot; smooth top with an offset spatula. Top with blueberries. Wrap lid with a clean kitchen towel, gathering the ends at top (to absorb condensation). Cover and cook on high for 2 hours (or on low for 4 hours); cake will be undercooked. Rotate halfway through for even baking. Make the Streusel: 4. In a small bowl, combine flour, brown sugar, butter, and cinnamon. Using a fork, mix butter into flour mixture until fine crumbs form. Using your hands, squeeze together the mixture to form large clumps. 5. Scatter streusel on top of cake, concentrating mixture around edges. Cover and cook on high until a tester inserted in center comes out clean, 1 to 1½ hours longer (or on low for 2 to 3 hours). Cool in pan for 15 minutes, then invert onto a cutting board; invert again onto a wire rack to cool completely, right side up.

Mom's Old-Fashioned Rice Pudding

Prep time: 10 minutes | Cook time: 2½ to 3 hours | Serves 6 to 8

- 5 cups whole milk
- 2 cups heavy cream
- 1¼ cups sugar
- 1 teaspoon vanilla bean paste
- ½ teaspoon freshly grated
- nutmeg
- 1 cup Arborio or other medium-grain rice, rinsed several times with cold water and drained

1. Coat the insert of a 5- to 7-quart crock pot with nonstick cooking spray. Whisk together the milk, cream, sugar, vanilla bean paste, and nutmeg in a large bowl and pour into the slow-cooker insert. Add the rice and stir to combine. 2. Cover and cook on low for 2½ to 3 hours, until the pudding is soft and creamy and the rice is tender. Remove the cover, turn off the cooker, and allow to cool for 30 minutes. 3. Serve warm, at room temperature, or chilled.

Red Wine Poached Pears with Stilton

Prep time: 10 minutes | Cook time: 2 to 2½ hours | Serves 6 to 8

- 1 cup full-bodied red wine
- 1 cup Ruby Port
- 1½ cups firmly packed light brown sugar
- 1 (4-inch) cinnamon stick
- 6 large firm red pears, halved and cored
- 6 ounces (170 g) Stilton cheese, at room temperature

1. Combine the wine, port, brown sugar, and cinnamon stick in the insert of a 5- to 7-quart crock pot. Add the pears to the slow-cooker insert, arranging them in layers, and spoon some of the sauce over the pears. 2. Cover and cook on high for 2 to 2½ hours, until the pears are softened. Uncover the crock pot and allow the pears to cool to room temperature. Carefully remove them from the cooker and arrange them on a platter. Strain the sauce through a fine-mesh sieve and boil for 5 to 10 minutes until the sauce becomes syrupy. 3. Spoon the syrup over the pears on the platter and scoop a bit of Stilton into the center of each pear. Serve at room temperature.

Sour Cream Amaretti Cheesecake

Prep time: 15 minutes | Cook time: 3 hours | Serves 6

- ¾ cup amaretti cookie crumbs (around 20 cookies, crushed)
- 2½ tablespoons unsalted butter, melted
- ½ teaspoon salt
- ¼ teaspoon ground cinnamon
- ⅓ cup granulated sugar,
- plus 1 tablespoon
- 12 ounces (340 g) cream cheese, at room temperature
- 1 tablespoon all-purpose flour
- 2 large eggs
- 1 teaspoon almond extract
- 1 cup sour cream

1. In a medium bowl, mix the cookie crumbs, melted butter, ¼ teaspoon of the salt, cinnamon, and 1 tablespoon sugar. Press the crumb mixture into a 6-inch springform pan, covering the bottom of pan and going about 1 inch up the side of the pan to form a crust. 2. With an electric mixer in a medium bowl, combine the cream cheese, flour, remaining ⅔ cup sugar, and remaining ¼ teaspoon salt. Beat at medium-high until smooth. 3. Scrape down the sides of bowl. Add the eggs and the almond extract. Beat until blended. 4. Add the sour cream and beat until smooth. 5. Pour the batter over the cookie crumb crust in the springform pan. 6. Fill the crock pot with ½ inch water and place the rack in the bottom, making sure the top of the rack is above the water. Set the springform pan with the cheesecake in it on the rack. Cover the crock pot with a triple layer of paper towels, and then cover with the lid. Cook on high for 2 hours without opening the crock pot even once. 7. Turn off the heat and let stand until cooker has cooled, again without opening lid, at least 1 additional hour. 8. Remove the cheesecake and chill for about 3 hours before serving in wedges.

Sour-Cream Cheesecake

Prep time: 10 minutes | Cook time: 5 to 6 hours | Serves 10

- ¼ cup butter, melted, divided
- 1 cup ground almonds
- ¾ cup plus 1 tablespoon granulated erythritol, divided
- ¼ teaspoon ground cinnamon
- 12 ounces (340 g) cream cheese, at room temperature
- 2 eggs
- 2 teaspoons pure vanilla extract
- 1 cup sour cream

1. Lightly grease a 7-inch springform pan with 1 tablespoon of the butter. 2. In a small bowl, stir together the almonds,

1 tablespoon of the erythritol, and cinnamon until blended. 3. Add the remaining 3 tablespoons of the butter and stir until coarse crumbs form. 4. Press the crust mixture into the springform pan along the bottom and about 2 inches up the sides. 5. In a large bowl, using a handheld mixer, beat together the cream cheese, eggs, vanilla, and remaining ¾ cup of the erythritol. Beat the sour cream into the cream-cheese mixture until smooth. 6. Spoon the batter into the springform pan and smooth out the top. 7. Place a wire rack in the insert of the crock pot and place the springform pan on top. 8. Cover and cook on low for 5 to 6 hours, or until the cheesecake doesn't jiggle when shaken. 9. Cool completely before removing from pan. 10. Chill the cheesecake completely before serving, and store leftovers in the refrigerator.

Fruit Dessert Topping

Prep time: 20 minutes | Cook time: 3½ to 4¾ hours | Makes 6 cups

- 3 tart apples, peeled and sliced
- 3 pears, peeled and sliced
- 1 tablespoon lemon juice
- ½ cup packed brown sugar
- ½ cup maple syrup
- ¼ cup butter, melted
- ½ cup chopped pecans
- ¼ cup raisins
- 2 cinnamon sticks
- 1 tablespoon cornstarch
- 2 tablespoons cold water

1. Toss apples and pears in lemon juice in crock pot. 2. Combine brown sugar, maple syrup, and butter. Pour over fruit. 3. Stir in pecans, raisins, and cinnamon sticks. 4. Cover. Cook on low 3 to 4 hours. 5. Combine cornstarch and water until smooth. Gradually stir into crock pot. 6. Cover. Cook on high 30 to 40 minutes, or until thickened. 7. Discard cinnamon sticks. Serve.

Pumpkin-Ginger Pudding

Prep time: 5 minutes | Cook time: 3 to 4 hours | Serves 8

- 1 tablespoon coconut oil
- 2 cups pumpkin purée
- 1½ cups coconut milk
- 2 eggs
- ½ cup almond flour
- 1 ounce (28 g) protein powder
- 1 tablespoon grated fresh ginger
- ¾ teaspoon liquid stevia
- Pinch ground cloves
- 1 cup whipped coconut cream

1. Lightly grease the insert of the crock pot with coconut oil. 2. In a large bowl, stir together pumpkin, coconut milk, eggs, almond flour, protein powder, ginger, liquid stevia, and cloves. 3. Transfer the mixture to the insert. 4. Cover and cook on low 3 to 4 hours. 5. Serve warm with whipped coconut cream.

Mixed Berry Clafoutis

Prep time: 15 minutes | Cook time: 2 hours | Serves 6

- 1 cup all-purpose flour
- 1¾ cups granulated sugar
- 1 teaspoon baking powder
- ¼ teaspoon salt
- ¼ teaspoon ground cinnamon
- ¼ teaspoon ground nutmeg
- 2 eggs, lightly beaten
- 3 teaspoons olive oil (not extra-virgin)
- 2 tablespoons milk
- 2 cups fresh blueberries
- 2 cups fresh raspberries
- 2 cups fresh blackberries
- 1 cup water
- 3 tablespoons uncooked quick-cooking tapioca
- Whipped cream, for serving

1. In a medium bowl, stir together the flour, ¾ cup of the sugar, baking powder, salt, cinnamon, and nutmeg. 2. In a small bowl, whisk together the eggs, olive oil, and milk. 3. Add the egg mixture to the flour mixture and stir to combine, just until moistened. Set aside. 4. In a large heavy saucepan over medium heat, combine the blueberries, raspberries, blackberries, the remaining 1 cup sugar, the water, and the tapioca. Bring to a boil. 5. Pour the hot fruit mixture into the crock pot. Immediately spoon the batter over the fruit mixture. 6. Cover and cook on high for 1¾ to 2 hours or until a toothpick inserted into the center of the cake topper comes out clean. 7. Remove the crock from the cooker, if possible, or uncover and turn off the cooker. Let stand, uncovered, for 1 hour to cool slightly. 8. To serve, spoon the warm clafoutis into dessert dishes and top with the whipped cream.

Apple-Pear Streusel

Prep time: 20 minutes | Cook time: 7 hours | Serves 2

- Nonstick cooking spray
- 4 apples, peeled and sliced
- 2 pears, peeled and sliced
- ¼ cup brown sugar
- 1 tablespoon freshly squeezed lemon juice
- ½ teaspoon ground cinnamon
- 2 tablespoons butter, plus 3 tablespoons cut into cubes, divided
- ½ cup light cream
- 1 cup all-purpose flour
- ½ cup rolled oats
- ½ cup chopped pecans
- ⅓ cup granulated sugar

1. Spray the crock pot with the nonstick cooking spray. 2. In the crock pot, combine the apple and pear slices; sprinkle with the brown sugar, lemon juice, and cinnamon, and mix. Dot with 2 tablespoons of butter and pour the cream over everything. 3. In a medium bowl, combine the flour, oats, pecans, and granulated sugar. Add the remaining 3 tablespoons of butter cubes, and cut in with two knives or a pastry blender until

crumbly. Sprinkle the mixture over the fruit. 4. Cover and cook on low for 7 hours, or until the fruit is tender.

Tempting Lemon Custard

Prep time: 10 minutes | Cook time: 3 hours | Serves 4

- 5 egg yolks
- ¼ cup freshly squeezed lemon juice
- 1 tablespoon lemon zest
- 1 teaspoon pure vanilla extract
- ⅓ teaspoon liquid stevia
- 2 cups heavy (whipping) cream
- 1 cup whipped coconut cream

1. In a medium bowl, whisk together the yolks, lemon juice and zest, vanilla, and liquid stevia. 2. Whisk in the heavy cream and divide the mixture between 4 (4-ounce / 113-g) ramekins. 3. Place a rack at the bottom of the insert of the crock pot and place the ramekins on it. 4. Pour in enough water to reach halfway up the sides of the ramekins. 5. Cover and cook on low for 3 hours. 6. Remove the ramekins from the insert and cool to room temperature. 7. Chill the ramekins completely in the refrigerator and serve topped with whipped coconut cream.

Maple Creme Brulee

Prep time: 20 minutes | Cook time: 2 hours | Serves 3

- 1⅓ cups heavy whipping cream
- 3 egg yolks
- ½ cup packed brown sugar
- ¼ teaspoon ground cinnamon
- ½ teaspoon maple flavoring
- Topping:
- 1½ teaspoons sugar
- 1½ teaspoons brown sugar

1. In a small saucepan, heat cream until bubbles form around sides of pan. In a small bowl, whisk the egg yolks, brown sugar and cinnamon. Remove cream from the heat; stir a small amount of hot cream into egg mixture. Return all to the pan, stirring constantly. Stir in maple flavoring. 2. Transfer to three 6-oz. ramekins or custard cups. Place in a 6-quart crock pot; add 1 inch of boiling water to crock pot. Cover and cook on high for 2 to 2½ hours or until centers are just set (mixture will jiggle). Carefully remove ramekins from crock pot; cool for 10 minutes. Cover and refrigerate for at least 4 hours. 3. For topping, combine sugar and brown sugar. If using a creme brulee torch, sprinkle custards with sugar mixture. Heat sugar with the torch until caramelized. Serve immediately. 4. If broiling the custards, place ramekins on a baking sheet; let stand at room temperature for 15 minutes. Sprinkle with sugar mixture. Broil 8 inch from the heat for 3 to 5 minutes or until sugar is caramelized. Refrigerate for 1 to 2 hours or until firm.

Blood Orange Upside-Down Cake

Prep time: 25 minutes | Cook time: 4 hours | Serves 6 to 8

- Orange Layer:
- 5 tablespoons unsalted butter, cut into small pieces, plus more for crock pot crock
- ¾ cup firmly packed dark brown sugar
- 3 tablespoons dark rum
- 2 pounds (907 g) blood oranges (about 6), sliced, peeled, with all of the bitter white pith removed
- ½ teaspoon ground cardamom
- Cake:
- ¾ cups cake flour
- ¾ teaspoons baking powder
- ½ teaspoon ground cinnamon
- ¼ teaspoon ground nutmeg
- ¼ teaspoon salt
- 4 tablespoons unsalted butter, at room temperature
- ⅔ cup granulated sugar
- 1 egg, at room temperature
- 1 egg yolk, at room temperature
- 2 tablespoons whole milk, at room temperature
- 2 cups vanilla ice cream, for serving (optional)

Make the Orange Layer: 1. Butter the inside of the crock pot crock, line completely with foil, and then butter the foil. 2. Sprinkle the butter, brown sugar, and rum over the foil on the bottom of the crock pot. Cover that with the orange slices in a slightly overlapping pattern, and sprinkle with the cardamom. Press the oranges into the sugar. Make the Cake: 3. Sift the flour, baking powder, cinnamon, nutmeg, and salt into a large bowl. Whisk gently to combine evenly. 4. In a medium bowl, slowly beat the butter and sugar with an electric mixer until just blended. Raise the speed to high and beat until light and fluffy, scraping down the sides of the bowl occasionally, about 10 minutes. 5. Beat the egg and then the egg yolk into the butter-sugar mixture, allowing each to be fully incorporated before adding the next. 6. While mixing slowly, add the flour mixture to the butter-sugar mixture in three parts, alternating with the milk in two parts, beginning and ending with the flour. Mix briefly at medium speed to make a smooth batter. 7. Pour the batter over the oranges in the crock pot and smooth with a spatula to even it out. 8. Lay a doubled length of paper towel from end to end over the top of the crock pot, to line the lid and create a tighter seal. 9. Cover the cake tightly with the lid and cook on high until the cake begins to brown slightly on the sides and springs back when touched in the middle, about 3½ hours. Turn off the crock pot and let the cake set, uncovered, about 20 minutes more. 10. Using the foil, lift the cake from the crock pot and set on the counter to cool, about 30 minutes more. Fold back the foil, and carefully invert the cake onto a platter so the caramelized oranges are visible on top. 11. Slice or spoon the cake into bowls, and serve with ice cream, if desired.

Apple Crisp

Prep time: 10 minutes | Cook time: 2 to 3 hours | Serves 6 to 8

- 1 quart canned apple pie filling
- ¾ cup quick oatmeal
- ½ cup brown sugar
- ½ cup flour
- ¼ cup butter, at room temperature

1. Place pie filling in crock pot. 2. Combine remaining ingredients until crumbly. Sprinkle over apple filling. 3. Cover. Cook on low 2 to 3 hours.

Apple Dish

Prep time: 20 minutes | Cook time: 2 to 2½ hours | Makes about 7 cups

- ¾ cup sugar
- 3 tablespoons flour
- 1½ teaspoons cinnamon (optional)
- 5 large baking apples, pared, cored, and diced into ¾-inch pieces
- Half a stick butter, melted
- 3 tablespoons water
- Nonstick cooking spray

1. Spray interior of crock pot with nonstick cooking spray. 2. In a large bowl, mix sugar and flour together, along with cinnamon if you wish. Set aside. 3. Mix apples, butter, and water together in crock pot. Gently stir in flour mixture until apples are well coated. 4. Cover and cook on high 1½ hours, and then on low 30 to 60 minutes, or until apples are done to your liking. 5. Serve.

Black Forest Cake

Prep time: 10 minutes | Cook time: 2 to 2½ hours | Serves 8 to 10

- 1 (20-ounce / 567-g) cherry pie filling (Lite or regular)
- 1 (18¼-ounce / 517-g) box butter-style chocolate cake mix
- Nonstick cooking spray

1. Preheat crock pot on high for 10 minutes. 2. Meanwhile, spray interior of baking insert, designed to fit into your crock pot, with nonstick cooking spray. 3. In a bowl, stir together pie filling and cake mix until mix is thoroughly moistened. Spoon into insert. 4. Place insert into cooker. Cover insert with 8 paper towels. Cover crock pot. 5. Cook on high 1¾ hours. Remove paper towels and cooker lid. Continue cooking for another 30 minutes, or until a toothpick inserted in the center of the cake comes out clean. 6. Remove baking insert from cooker. Serve cake warm directly from the insert.

Brandied Peaches

Prep time: 10 minutes | Cook time: 2 hours | Serves 8

- ½ cup brandy
- ½ cup (1 stick) unsalted butter, melted
- 1½ cups firmly packed light brown sugar
- 2 (4-inch) cinnamon sticks
- 4 whole cloves
- ½ cup peach nectar
- 8 large large peaches, peeled, halved, and pitted

1. Combine the brandy, butter, sugar, cinnamon sticks, cloves, and nectar in the insert of a 5- to 7-quart crock pot and stir to dissolve the sugar. Add the peaches to the slow-cooker insert and turn to coat them with the syrup. 2. Cover and cook on high for 2 hours. Allow the peaches to cool slightly. Using a slotted spoon, remove the spices from the sauce. 3. Serve the peaches with the sauce poured over.

Apple-Pear Sauce

Prep time: 20 minutes | Cook time: 8 hours | Makes 8 cups

- Nonstick cooking spray
- 4 apples, peeled and sliced
- 3 firm pears, peeled and sliced
- ¼ cup apple cider
- ½ cup granulated sugar
- 2 tablespoons freshly
- squeezed lemon juice
- 1 teaspoon ground cinnamon
- 1 teaspoon ground nutmeg
- ⅛ teaspoon salt
- 1 teaspoon vanilla

1. Spray the crock pot with the nonstick cooking spray. 2. In the crock pot, combine the apples and pears, and stir. 3. Add the apple cider, sugar, lemon juice, cinnamon, nutmeg, and salt, and mix. 4. Cover and cook on low for 7 to 8 hours, or until the fruit is very soft. 5. Using a fork or potato masher, mash the mixture to the desired consistency. Stir in the vanilla and remove from the crock pot. 6. Serve immediately or cool and then refrigerate for up to 4 days or freeze.

Chocolate Rice Pudding

Prep time: 10 minutes | Cook time: 2½ to 3½ hours | Serves 4

- 4 cups white rice, cooked
- ¾ cup sugar
- ¼ cup baking cocoa powder
- 3 tablespoons butter, melted
- 1 teaspoon vanilla
- 2 (12-ounce / 340-g) cans evaporated milk
- Whipped cream
- Sliced toasted almonds
- Maraschino cherries

1. Combine first 6 ingredients in greased crock pot. 2. Cover. Cook on low 2½ to 3½ hours, or until liquid is absorbed. 3. Serve warm or chilled. Top individual servings with a dollop of whipped cream, sliced toasted almonds, and a maraschino cherry.

Hot Fudge Cake

Prep time: 10 minutes | Cook time: 1½ to 1¾ hours | Serves 8

- 1¾ cups brown sugar, divided
- 1 cup flour
- 3 tablespoons, plus ¼ cup, unsweetened cocoa, divided
- 1½ teaspoons baking powder
- ½ teaspoon salt
- ½ cup skim milk
- 2 tablespoons butter, melted
- ½ teaspoon vanilla
- 1¾ cups boiling water
- Nonfat cooking spray

1. In a mixing bowl, mix together 1 cup brown sugar, flour, 3 tablespoons cocoa, baking powder, and salt. 2. Stir in milk, butter, and vanilla. 3. Pour into crock pot sprayed with nonfat cooking spray. 4. In a separate bowl, mix together ¾ cup brown sugar and ¼ cup cocoa. Sprinkle over batter in the crock pot. Do not stir. 5. Pour boiling water over mixture. Do not stir. 6. Cover. Cook on high 1½ to 1¾ hours, or until toothpick inserted into cake comes out clean.

Blackberry Cobbler

Prep time: 15 minutes | Cook time: 3 to 4 hours | Serves 10

- Filling:
- 1 tablespoon coconut oil
- 6 cups blackberries
- ½ cup granulated erythritol
- 1 teaspoon ground cinnamon
- Topping:
- 2 cups ground almonds
- ½ cup granulated erythritol
- 1 tablespoon baking powder
- ½ teaspoon salt
- 1 cup heavy (whipping) cream
- ½ cup butter, melted

Make the Filling: 1. Lightly grease the insert of a 4-quart crock pot with the coconut oil. 2. Add the blackberries, erythritol, and cinnamon to the insert. Mix to combine. Make the Topping: 3. In a large bowl, stir together the almonds, erythritol, baking powder, and salt. Add the heavy cream and butter and stir until a thick batter forms. 4. Drop the batter by the tablespoon on top of the blackberries. 5. Cover and cook on low for 3 to 4 hours. 6. Serve warm.

Chapter 10

Pizzas, Wraps, and Sandwiches

Hawaiian Sausage Subs

Prep time: 15 minutes | Cook time: 3 hours | Serves 12

- 3 pounds (1.4 kg) smoked kielbasa or Polish sausage, cut into 3-inch pieces
- 2 (12-ounce / 340-g) bottles chili sauce
- 1 (20-ounce / 567-g) can pineapple tidbits, undrained
- ¼ cup packed brown sugar
- 12 hoagie buns, split

1. Place kielbasa in a 3-quart crock pot. Combine the chili sauce, pineapple and brown sugar; pour over kielbasa. Cover and cook on low for 3 to 4 hours or until heated through. Serve on buns.

Barbecued Ham Sandwiches

Prep time: 7 minutes | Cook time: 5 hours | Makes 4 to 6 sandwiches

- 1 pound (454 g) chipped turkey ham or chipped honey-glazed ham
- 1 small onion, finely diced
- ½ cup ketchup
- 1 tablespoon vinegar
- 3 tablespoons brown sugar
- Buns, for serving

1. Place half of meat in greased crock pot. 2. Combine other ingredients. Pour half of mixture over meat. Repeat layers. 3. Cover. Cook on low 5 hours. 4. Fill buns and serve.

Beef and Veggie Sloppy Joes

Prep time: 35 minutes | Cook time: 5 hours | Serves 12

- 4 medium carrots, shredded (about 3½ cups)
- 1 medium yellow summer squash, shredded (about 2 cups)
- 1 medium zucchini, shredded (about 2 cups)
- 1 medium sweet red pepper, finely chopped
- 2 medium tomatoes, seeded and chopped
- 1 small red onion, finely chopped
- ½ cup ketchup
- 3 tablespoons minced fresh basil or 3 teaspoons dried basil
- 3 tablespoons molasses
- 2 tablespoons cider vinegar
- 2 garlic cloves, minced
- ½ teaspoon salt
- ½ teaspoon pepper
- 2 pounds (907 g) lean ground beef (90% lean)
- 12 whole wheat hamburger buns, split

1. In a 5- or 6-quart crock pot, combine the first 13 ingredients. In a large skillet, cook beef over medium heat 8 to 10 minutes or until no longer pink, breaking into crumbles. Drain; transfer beef to crock pot. Stir to combine. 2. Cook, covered, on low 5

to 6 hours or until heated through and vegetables are tender. Using a slotted spoon, serve beef mixture on buns.

Enchilada Pie

Prep time: 40 minutes | Cook time: 4 hours | Serves 8

- 1 (12-ounce / 340-g) package frozen vegetarian meat crumbles
- 1 cup chopped onion
- ½ cup chopped green pepper
- 2 teaspoons canola oil
- 1 (16-ounce / 454-g) can kidney beans, rinsed and drained
- 1 (15-ounce / 425-g) can black beans, rinsed and
- drained
- 1 (10-ounce / 283-g) can diced tomatoes and green chilies, undrained
- ½ cup water
- 1½ teaspoons chili powder
- ½ teaspoon ground cumin
- ¼ teaspoon pepper
- 6 whole wheat tortillas
- 2 cups shredded reduced-fat cheddar cheese

1. Cut three 25x3-inch strips of heavy-duty foil; crisscross so they resemble spokes of a wheel. Place strips on the bottom and up the sides of a 5-quart crock pot. Coat strips with cooking spray. 2. In a large saucepan, cook the meat crumbles, onion and green pepper in oil until vegetables are tender. Stir in both cans of beans, tomatoes, water, chili powder, cumin and pepper. Bring to a boil. Reduce heat; simmer, uncovered, for 10 minutes. 3. In prepared crock pot, layer about a cup of bean mixture, one tortilla and ⅓ cup cheese. Repeat layers five times. Cover and cook on low for 4 to 5 hours or until heated through and cheese is melted. 4. Using foil strips as handles, remove the pie to a platter.

Herby French Sandwiches

Prep time: 5 minutes | Cook time: 5 to 6 hours | Makes 6 to 8 sandwiches

- 1 (3-pound / 1.4-kg) chuck roast
- 2 cups water
- ½ cup soy sauce
- 1 teaspoon garlic powder
- 1 bay leaf
- 3 to 4 whole peppercorns
- 1 teaspoon dried rosemary (optional)
- 1 teaspoon dried thyme (optional)
- 6 to 8 French rolls

1. Place roast in crock pot. 2. Combine remaining ingredients in a mixing bowl. Pour over meat. 3. Cover and cook on high 5 to 6 hours, or until meat is tender but not dry. 4. Remove meat from broth and shred with fork. Stir back into sauce. 5. Remove meat from the cooker by large forkfuls and place on French rolls.

Barbecue Sauce and Hot Beef Sandwiches

Prep time: 10 minutes | Cook time: 8 to 10 hours | Makes 10 sandwiches

- 3 pounds (1.4 kg) beef chuck roast
- 1 large onion, chopped
- ¼ cup vinegar
- 1 clove garlic, minced
- 1 to 1½ teaspoons salt
- ¼ to ½ teaspoon pepper
- Hamburger buns, for serving

1. Place meat in crock pot. Top with onions. 2. Combine vinegar, garlic, salt, and pepper. Pour over meat. 3. Cover. Cook on low 8 to 10 hours. 4. Drain broth but save for dipping. 5. Shred meat. 6. Serve on hamburger buns with broth on side.

Wash-Day Sandwiches

Prep time: 10 minutes | Cook time: 6 to 7 hours | Makes 8 to 10 sandwiches

- 1½ to 2 pounds (680 to 907 g) lean lamb or beef, cubed
- 2 (15-ounce / 425-g) cans garbanzo beans, drained
- 2 (15-ounce / 425-g) cans white beans, drained
- 2 medium onions, peeled and quartered
- 1 quart water
- 1 teaspoon salt
- 1 tomato, peeled and quartered
- 1 teaspoon turmeric
- 3 tablespoons fresh lemon juice
- 8 to 10 pita bread pockets

1. Combine ingredients in crock pot. 2. Cover. Cook on high 6 to 7 hours. 3. Lift stew from cooker with a strainer spoon and stuff in pita bread pockets.

Hamburgers

Prep time: 25 minutes | Cook time: 5 to 6 hours | Makes 6 sandwiches

- 1 (14¾-ounce / 418-g) can beef gravy
- ½ cup ketchup
- ½ cup chili sauce
- 1 tablespoon
- Worcestershire sauce
- 1 tablespoon prepared mustard
- 6 grilled hamburger patties
- 6 slices cheese (optional)

1. Combine all ingredients except hamburger patties and cheese slices in crock pot. 2. Add hamburger patties. 3. Cover. Cook on low 5 to 6 hours. 4. Serve in buns, each topped with a slice of cheese if you like.

Tangy Barbecue Sandwiches

Prep time: 20 minutes | Cook time: 7 to 9 hours | Makes 14 to 18 sandwiches

- 3 cups chopped celery
- 1 cup chopped onions
- 1 cup ketchup
- 1 cup barbecue sauce
- 1 cup water
- 2 tablespoons vinegar
- 2 tablespoons Worcestershire sauce
- 2 tablespoons brown sugar
- 1 teaspoon chili powder
- 1 teaspoon salt
- ½ teaspoon pepper
- ½ teaspoon garlic powder
- 1 (3- to 4-pound / 1.4- to 1.8-kg) boneless chuck roast
- 14 to 18 hamburger buns

1. Combine all ingredients except roast and buns in crock pot. When well mixed, add roast. 2. Cover. Cook on high 6 to 7 hours. 3. Remove roast. Cool and shred meat. Return to sauce. Heat well. 4. Serve on buns.

Easy Philly Cheese Steaks

Prep time: 20 minutes | Cook time: 6 hours | Serves 6

- 2 medium onions, halved and sliced
- 2 medium sweet red or green peppers, halved and sliced
- 1 (1½-pound / 680-g) beef top sirloin steak, cut into thin strips
- 1 envelope onion soup mix
- 1 (14½-ounce / 411-g) can reduced-sodium beef broth
- 6 hoagie buns, split
- 12 slices provolone cheese, halved
- Pickled hot cherry peppers (optional)

1. Place onions and red peppers in a 4- or 5-quart crock pot. Add the beef, soup mix and broth. Cook, covered, on low 6 to 8 hours or until the meat is tender. 2. Arrange buns on a baking sheet, cut side up. Using tongs, place meat mixture on bun bottoms; top with cheese. 3. Broil 2 to 3 inch from heat 30 to 60 seconds or until cheese is melted and bun tops are toasted. If desired, serve with cherry peppers.

Appendix ①

Measurement Conversion Chart

VOLUME EQUIVALENTS(DRY)

US STANDARD	METRIC (APPROXIMATE)
1/8 teaspoon	0.5 mL
1/4 teaspoon	1 mL
1/2 teaspoon	2 mL
3/4 teaspoon	4 mL
1 teaspoon	5 mL
1 tablespoon	15 mL
1/4 cup	59 mL
1/2 cup	118 mL
3/4 cup	177 mL
1 cup	235 mL
2 cups	475 mL
3 cups	700 mL
4 cups	1 L

VOLUME EQUIVALENTS(LIQUID)

US STANDARD	US STANDARD (OUNCES)	METRIC (APPROXIMATE)
2 tablespoons	1 fl.oz.	30 mL
1/4 cup	2 fl.oz.	60 mL
1/2 cup	4 fl.oz.	120 mL
1 cup	8 fl.oz.	240 mL
1 1/2 cup	12 fl.oz.	355 mL
2 cups or 1 pint	16 fl.oz.	475 mL
4 cups or 1 quart	32 fl.oz.	1 L
1 gallon	128 fl.oz.	4 L

TEMPERATURES EQUIVALENTS

FAHRENHEIT(F)	CELSIUS(C) (APPROXIMATE)
225 °F	107 °C
250 °F	120 °C
275 °F	135 °C
300 °F	150 °C
325 °F	160 °C
350 °F	180 °C
375 °F	190 °C
400 °F	205 °C
425 °F	220 °C
450 °F	235 °C
475 °F	245 °C
500 °F	260 °C

WEIGHT EQUIVALENTS

US STANDARD	METRIC (APPROXIMATE)
1 ounce	28 g
2 ounces	57 g
5 ounces	142 g
10 ounces	284 g
15 ounces	425 g
16 ounces (1 pound)	455 g
1.5 pounds	680 g
2 pounds	907 g

Appendix ②

Index

Made in United States
Orlando, FL
24 November 2024

54383570R00052